DATE DUE

MY LSE

Other titles in this series (General Editor: Dannie Abse)

MY OXFORD

MY CAMBRIDGE

Forthcoming:

MY DRAMA SCHOOL

MY MEDICAL SCHOOL

MY LSE

CHAIM BERMANT   BERNARD CRICK   COLIN CROUCH
AUBREY JONES   NORMAN MACKENZIE
ROBERT McKENZIE   KENNETH MINOGUE   RON MOODY
B. K. NEHRU   J. W. N. WATKINS   JACQUELINE WHELDON
KRISHENDATH MAHARAJ   FREDERIC C. WEISS

Edited and introduced by
JOAN ABSE

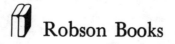 Robson Books

FIRST PUBLISHED IN GREAT BRITAIN IN 1977
BY ROBSON BOOKS LTD., 28 POLAND STREET,
LONDON W1V 3DB. COPYRIGHT © 1977 ROBSON
BOOKS

MY LSE
1. London School of Economics and Political Science—
                        History
I. Abse, Joan
330'.07'1142132   LF449.L9

ISBN 0-86051-014-X

Printed and bound in Great Britain by R. J. Acford Ltd,
                    Chichester, Sussex

CONTENTS

INTRODUCTION

Jf history is the essence of innumerable biographies as
Carlyle averred, I think it can be claimed that at least a
few drams of the historical spirit of LSE is distilled in the
autobiographical fragments to be found in these pages. Indeed,
it seems to me that quite a significant part of the history of the
School since its inception in 1895 can be seen in biographical
terms. The idea may seem paradoxical; after all, LSE is known
as an institution devoting itself, for the most part, to non-
subjective investigation. Yet the institution itself indisputably
is part of the biography of the founders, Sidney and Beatrice
Webb, and the sequence of events leading to the foundation
relate to the eccentric life of another individual whose name
has faded but whose actions were seminal. This was Henry
Hutchinson, former clerk to the Derby magistrates and an
earnest Fabian, who shot himself in 1894 and left £10,000 to
Sidney Webb, whom he had never even met, for the purpose of
aiding the Fabian Society and spreading Socialist propaganda.
Webb, already dissatisfied with the state of economic teaching
in this country, proved himself a man of some imagination
when he saw that this money together with funds and donations
from other sources, could be used to found a School which
would systematically study economic and social problems. Such
study might or might not further the Fabian case for Socialism
—Sidney Webb was inclined to believe that it would—but, as

Janet Beveridge in her account of the history of the School put it, 'Most happily for Sidney the objects of the Society included advancing the understanding of economics.'

When LSE's subsequent history is considered, it seems to me clear that it was to the teaching of remarkable and dedicated men and women that its reputation became due. Graham Wallas, R. H. Tawney, Beveridge, Eileen Power—these are but a few of the names that spring to mind. Of course, it may be argued that it is natural that it should be so; on what should a university depend but on the learning of its teachers and their capacity to pass on that learning to the young. In fact, it is clear that this is not always the case, that the older universities, for example, offer more than their curriculum and its teachers; they offer besides a tradition, a prestige, and a particularly pleasing environment. LSE was and remains different. It depended on the merits of its teachers and what they sought to teach. Triumphantly it succeeded and continues to succeed so that students from all parts of the world clamour to enter.

So gratitude for teaching received is a constant theme within these pages—appropriately enough in a volume devoted to university reminiscences. (Even Chaim Bermant who amazingly and defiantly begins his piece, 'I hated the place', has to admit that he has only praise for the teaching he encountered.) The longest, and clearly most deeply felt eulogies are reserved for Harold Laski who, at one time, seemed to epitomize LSE to so many people. By students he seems, as these memoirs witness, to have been universally admired, even beloved, though perhaps few followed him uncritically. In the days of the 1945 election when he was being represented to the country as the incarnation of the 'red' menace, I personally as a young student found him much too 'pink'. I remember vividly his kindly Shakespearean put-down—there is 'much virtue in "if" '—after I had harangued him on one occasion on the probable imminence of the millenium. Stories abound about him yet he is only the most egregious among many whose virtues are recorded here.

It may be that Laski, more than anyone, as Robert McKenzie declares, was responsible for the myth of 'red' LSE which several contributors to this book are anxious to explode. Nevertheless accusations of it being socialist inclined gathered about LSE, perhaps not unnaturally, from its beginnings, and though the staff may have become less and less radical, the same is not true for the student body. It is not hard to see why this should be so for many students who entered, and still enter, LSE seek to study society and its workings because they are profoundly dissatisfied with existing arrangements. Just as the Webbs believed that socialism could provide the answer to the irrational and unjust aspects of society, and hoped that a study of economics and politics would show the merits of socialist solutions, so many students have been led to LSE for the very same reasons, and once there have identified themselves as lively exponents of one shade or another of the 'red' cause.

Certainly this was the reason why I went to LSE. I went imbued with an emotional conviction that the world needed changing coupled with an appreciation that it might be useful, as well as fascinating, to learn more about its social ramifications before I applied myself to the business of changing it. By the time I had finished my studies at LSE my aspirations no longer seemed so clear-cut and my ambitions were much more circumscribed. However, I think it is the feeling which so many students possess of burning concern with current political and social problems and ambitions to deal with them which helps to give LSE its unique flavour. 'You LSE people, you always set yourselves apart and talk as if you were some special incestuous race,' one of Jay Wheldon's Oxford friends accused her some years ago; the charge has some truth in it and I think it is the sense of their heightened political awareness which contributes to make many LSE students believe that they belong to a special fraternity.

Perhaps another reason is to be found in the wide variety of students gathered together, all bent on related studies. A large number are postgraduate students and this element is repre-

sented in this volume. Equally a considerable number are from
overseas, many from the Third World, and they combine to
give the School a decided cosmopolitan feeling. Some of these
students have returned home to achieve positions of eminence
in their own countries. I have been fortunate enough to receive
a contribution from the present Indian High Commissioner
who was at LSE very nearly half a century ago, while Krishendath Maharaj, from Trinidad, a present-day student, interestingly brings the picture up to date. (Noticing the troubles that
have beset LSE in recent months over the imposition of increased fees which particularly affects overseas and postgraduate students, I decided to ask two students with somewhat
different points of view to contribute their up-to-date impres-
sions to the book.)

My own memories of LSE are very much bound up with my
encounter with students from other countries, many of them
older and of wide experience, some of them refugees from the
tyrannies of Europe. Like Norman MacKenzie, I was fortunate
enough to go there during the war (though there seems a
terrible irony in that remark) when it was evacuated to Cambridge and was indeed what Professor MacKenzie felicitously
terms 'a student utopia'. Though, in 1943, when I first went to
LSE, the war seemed endless, Cambridge was like a delightful
oasis of happiness and fulfilment in a world bent on destruction.
LSE in Cambridge was an ideal place in which student life
could flourish. The older, enriching virtues of Cambridge were
leavened by the easy-going, lively, unconventional atmosphere
of the School. We could enjoy the captivating beauty of the
place without, as most of us saw it, the disadvantages of segregated college life. Even the rigours of Cambridge landladies,
who always preferred men students because they did not insist
on doing their washing, were preferable to that. And many of us
managed somehow to find our own flats where we could try
out, with our limited rations and varying degrees of success, the
foreign dishes which students from overseas were happy to
teach us.

I arrived from one of the dirtiest towns in Lancashire when I was barely seventeen with an embarrassing child's green ration book on which, I seem to remember, you could get special issues of bananas when they were available. At a time when 'Open up the Second Front' was on everyone's lips, I was a member of the anti-war ILP and full of pacifist zeal. Soon after my arrival and a fairly timid announcement of my views at a meeting of Soc. Soc on the situation in Greece, I was accused by a particularly flamboyant Persian Communist student of bringing the dread black banners of anarchism into the LSE stronghold. But LSE was capable of embracing a multitude of idiosyncracies and mine proved no exception.

There were no preliminary interviews in those wartime days. Everything was arranged by post according to examination qualifications. The war continued, the staff were dwindling, there was, perhaps, a certain irrelevance in our sheltered, university life, and consequently I do not remember any undue academic pressure in that intermediate time. Certainly I recollect many hours spent in the University Library following my own particular hobby horses—still, I think, an ideal way of pursuing one's education, though probably not for examination purposes. Laski's Saturday morning lectures, and even more, his seminars and tutorials, were the high spots of the week. Another draw was Bertrand Russell, Cambridge not LSE, but still sufficiently involved with its foundation to be part of its history. Professor Hayek's lecture on economics often defeated me (do I dream or did he really stand on chairs or pile them on top of each other to illustrate his points?) and I fled to the inspired lucidity of Cambridge's Joan Robinson. Like others in this book, I also remember with gratitude the urbane teaching of Mr William Pickles and Mr Smellie, while in the field of applied economics with which I could always cope more satisfactorily than with the theory, I was glad of the lectures of Dr Lewis (now Sir Arthur Lewis) on labour relations, a subject which to me (Ruskinian to the core) seemed to be getting down to the real stuff of economics.

More than anything, however, what remains with me of my memories of LSE is the enriching company of my peers. It was thus with some dismay that I found B. K. Nehru recollects having little contact with English students during his life there in the early 1930s—even though he did reject his father's advice and marry a white woman; and I can only hope that Krishendath Maharaj will soon overcome the difficulty he finds in forming friendships with British students. For myself I recollect no difficult barriers to such friendships and I hope it was not because I was insensitive to them. Nor do I think it was because we all lived in such proximity in Cambridge, for some of my closest friendships were formed during my last year which was spent in London getting acquainted with LSE's true environment.

Equally uncharacteristic of my own experience do I find Frederic Weiss's description of LSE's present-day asexual attitudes. I hope he has just been unlucky. My impression was that most students took sex, with all its hazards and rewards, in their stride as a natural part of existence, though not everyone had the same level of curiosity as Robert McKenzie's Australian friend. The fact that three contributors, Norman MacKenzie, John Watkins and Colin Crouch, married fellow students I think proves my point. And there is Ron Moody's description of frustrated passion as evidence that the path of true love can, like everywhere else, be beset with torments. It just goes to show, however, that everyone's LSE is undoubtedly his own, and the LSE breed can display innumerable biographical varieties however often it may be suggested there is one particular genus.

JOAN ABSE

B. K. Nehru

Braj Kumar Nehru was born in Allahabad in 1909 and went to the London School of Economics in 1929. He was also educated at Allahabad University; Balliol College, Oxford; and was called to the Bar, Inner Temple. He joined the Indian Civil Service in 1934 and served in several departments of Government. From 1945 onwards he represented India at several international conferences and at the United Nations General Assembly from 1949–52. In 1946 he was deputed to enquire into Australian Federal Finance and in 1955 was adviser to the Sudan Government. He was Ambassador to the USA 1961–68 and since 1973 has been Indian High Commissioner in London. His publications include Speaking of India and Australian Federal Finance.

I was nineteen and a half, having just taken a degree from the University of Allahabad, my home town, in Physics, Chemistry and Mathematics, when in June 1929 I was shipped off to England for 'further studies'. I was despatched without any kind of arrangement having been made for my admission to any college or university. My father gave me a few letters of introduction and two prohibitions. 'You can read what you like and where you like but do not go to Oxford or Cambridge. And do not marry a white woman'. (As was to be expected I eventually did both!—though with his permission.) My father had himself spent six years at Oxford so the first prohibition sounded somewhat strange. But he explained that these older universities did not train people for 'the kind of life you will live in India, which' he said with prophetic wisdom 'will be very different from what it is now.'

I wished to study Economics and Political Science. I applied for admission to the LSE and was peremptorily rejected. The High Commission got me admitted, instead, to the University of Nottingham. It so happened that on a social occasion I met Sir Clive (later Lord) Wigram who was then Private Secretary to the King. He asked me to which university I was going and I said Nottingham. 'Nottingham?' he shouted 'NOTTINGHAM? What! You want to study lace-making or something? Why aren't you going to Oxford or Cambridge?' The position having

8

been explained he exploded again: 'Nonsense. NONSENSE!' But
then he calmed down and said: 'That William Beveridge owes
me a good turn or two. Let me see what I can do.' His unsought
intervention, together with that of some other friends of Sir
William, was how I began my four-year sojourn at the School—
a rather early education in the truth that whom you know is
more important than what you know!

I lost no time, long before the opening of term, in contacting
Professor Laski, by whom I was received with the utmost
courtesy and who gave me then, and throughout my stay, more
personal attention and more affection than my academic or
other achievements ever deserved. I remember well that he
told me to read, before term opened and as a preparation for
the study of Political Science, Bagehot's *English Constitution*,
Locke on *Toleration* and Burke's *Reflections on the French Revolution*.
Why he should have made this particular selection out of the
immense literature on political philosophy I was not then, and
am not now, at all certain. But so taken was I with him that
read them I did.

The manner in which the training of young minds was
organized in the School was very different from that to which
I had been used in India. In the Indian universities then—and
in most, undoubtedly, even now—there were a number of
text-books prescribed which you had to read, a series of
lectures which you had compulsorily to attend and periodical
examinations which you were obliged to pass. As long as you
paid a modicum of attention to your lectures and read enough
of your text-books you ultimately got your degree without
necessarily straying much beyond the path which had been
chalked out for you by your mentors. The organization of life
and learning was very much on the same pattern as at school;
there was a little greater freedom, some relaxation of discipline,
but in essence no greater demand on your own independent
thought processes nor much need of making your own decisions
or coming to your own conclusions. As long as you could repeat,
at the final examination, what the authorities on the subject had

said—not forgetting of course your own teachers!—you were regarded as a good student. 'Why don't you ever say,' Laski once said to me, 'in your answer papers, as your compatriots always do, "As the great Professor Laski has said" and then quote from my books?' To which the truthful answer—though I am sure I didn't give it—was that I had never been able to wade through *A Grammar of Politics*, for Laski's writing I found as turgidly convoluted as his lectures were brilliantly lucid.

In my new surroundings I suffered from an unwonted freedom to do what I wanted—a freedom I soon began shamelessly to abuse. I had of course to choose, for Part I of the degree, a certain number of subjects. There was a course of lectures attached to each subject and I presume one was expected to attend them but I do not recall—although one had to sign one's name in the class-room—that attendance was compulsory. I doubt very much that it was, for I soon developed the habit, which I fear grew worse as time went on, of cutting classes. There is an entry in a diary which I intermittently and sketchily kept at the time—which reads as follows: 'I had three lectures to attend today but attended only one. I played for the LSE against Battersea Polytechnic in a cup match.' (There are others in a similar vein and would have been many more had the diary been more regularly kept and a routine occurrence been regarded as worth recording!)

There was, further, the disconcerting absence of prescribed text-books. Each lecturer recommended a long list of books to read; in addition there was suggested at the end of many lectures material for further study in the shape of chapters of yet more books or articles in academic journals and magazines. The volume of recommended reading was so enormous that it was impossible for even the most diligent to do what had been asked. Some of my colleagues did attempt this task but succumbed sometimes to the danger of converting their minds into a chaos of undigested and uncoordinated information. My own response was the typically lazy one of drastically limiting my reading to what I considered to be the essentials which my mind could digest, leaving the finer points to be mastered by those with more acute understanding. A consequence of this procedure was that the lectures and the reading became somewhat uncoordinated, sometimes the one running ahead or lagging behind the other. But at some time they must have succeeded in catching each other up for I did manage always somehow to get through examinations and even got an honours degree!

My most shameful abuse of my new-found freedom was to stay in bed almost till midday. I am one of those unfortunates who find it impossible to get out of bed in the mornings and equally impossible to get back into it at night. This tendency, unless kept in check through external influence—a parent, a schoolmaster or a wife—can be carried to absurd extremes. And so it was during the entire time I was at the School. I started getting up later and later; arrival at the School before noon (except on Wednesdays for Laski's seminar) was the exception rather than the rule. I did usually manage to attend such lectures as were held in the afternoon—I had soon discovered that many courses of lectures were repeated in the evenings. And though I continued to pay my fees as a day student—they were higher than for evening classes—I became in effect an evening student. The library used to remain open till 9.30 pm and many an evening found me being thrown out of it when I had just got into my stride! There was then an hour or two or, exceptionally even three, of quiet reading in my digs. The entries in my diary were made invariably between 1 and 4 am! And on Saturday afternoons there was a longer period of voluntary study in the library.

To guide and help me in my first year through this welter of learning there was Vera Anstey. She was technically, I think, merely a lecturer in Commerce but she had been given or had taken upon herself a general motherly responsibility for all foreign students and she interpreted her task as being specially related to Indian students. I remember I wrote many essays for her, which she used, with great gentleness and tenderness, to

educate me in the elements of economic science, of which I was
totally ignorant but which, in the brashness of youth, I thought
I knew all about! Another guide—and one whose influence
continued all the years I was at LSE—was Harold Laski. My
special subject was Government and I was privileged, even
in my first year, to attend his seminars. These started at 12 noon
on Wednesdays in a building on the opposite side of Houghton
Street from the main building, and this was one day in the
week when I arrived on time. I was, by convention, allotted a
seat very near him and the proceedings started invariably with
his request 'Nehru, a cigarette.' Whereupon I produced from
my hip pocket a flat box of 50—this packaging disappeared
long ago—of Three Castles cigarettes—the yellow and cheaper
variety as opposed to the green! We lit up and the proceedings
commenced.

These consisted of the victim of the day reading his paper, for
the preparation of which he had had long notice, and the rest
of us, fifteen or so we were, tore it to shreds. Laski did not act as a
neutral chairman, as merely a ringmaster ensuring fair play
among the contestants, but very much as a participant and a
partisan, not minding in the least getting from his students
as good as he gave. I recall my own turn as a victim on one
occasion when the thesis I propounded with (for once) a
wealth of learning was that Lenin was anti-Marx, that he had
stood Marx on his head, had not waited for the development of
capitalism in Russia, let alone its contradictions, and had
created a revolution when the objective conditions for it, far
from being ripe, had not even begun to exist. So blasphemous a
thesis was hardly likely to be accepted by the Faithful, and I
found myself in a minority of one with Laski leading the attack!

But these seminars and his lectures were not the only sources
of his influence. I was among the privileged few who were per-
mitted to go, when we willed, to his Sunday soirées at his home
in Addison Bridge Place. These were visited, in addition to a few
favoured students, by many categories of people—foreign
visitors to London, politicians and academics—and Laski used

to hold forth, in the same style as he did at his lectures, humorous and caustic, regaling us with anecdotes of the mighty and setting forth his views, in no uncertain terms, on the problems and the personalities of the day. Among these the political situation in India, in which Laski took very genuine interest, was not an infrequent topic of discussion; on this, with my political connections, I was the expert! The Simon Commission on Indian Constitutional Reforms had been earlier sent to India. It had been boycotted by the Indian National Congress; had issued its report which had been rejected by India. The Salt Satyagraha had been started; a large number of my friends and relations were in jail; the sessions of the Round Table Conference were held and Mahatma Gandhi came to London from prison—to go back to it shortly after his return. An exciting—and harrowing—time for any Indian, particularly one like me, coming from an intensely political background.

Nor was the Indian situation by any means the only political development in the world which engrossed the attention of the LSE. The stockmarket had collapsed in New York in 1929; the Great Depression spread rapidly throughout the world. The Labour Government in Britain could not prevent a massive growth of unemployment in the country. Sterling was devalued; a National Government was formed—much to the disgust of the Left Wing of the Labour Party. Mussolini and the Fascists were ruling Italy. Hitler was rising to power and Oswald Mosley was building up quite a following in England. Japan had invaded Manchuria without the League of Nations doing anything about it, giving a signal to Mussolini to carve himself an empire in Africa. England was rapidly disarming. The Established Order was being challenged and could provide no response.

Young people tend naturally to be radical; equally naturally they tend to sympathize with Left- rather than Right-wing solutions. Believing in the essential goodness of human nature they assume that the former involve less exploitation of man by man. The students of the LSE were then extremely Left-wing—

the large majority were socialists or communists; so was the
Political Science Department, which dominated our thinking
rather than the Economics Department which was always more
conservative. Indian students in particular were all Left-wing;
the more extreme they were the more patriotic they were
considered to be. The explanation was simple: the burning
issue for us was Indian independence; the socialists and
communists supported it; the capitalists and Conservatives
opposed it. Ergo, socialism (or communism) was good; capitalism bad. This was also the period of the starry-eyed admiration of the intellectuals of the West for the Soviet Union. I
remember reading from cover to cover the Webbs' two volumes
on the New Civilization.

A couple of years ago there was a joke floating round the UN
in New York that when the whole world had developed and
become very rich, four countries would still remain under-
developed and poor. 'Which?' 'India, Sri Lanka, Bangladesh
and . . . the United Kingdom.' 'Why?' 'Because they all follow
policies advocated by the London School of Economics!' The
accusation was unfair to the Department of Economics, the
main thrust of whose teaching, in my time at least, could not
possibly be held responsible for the non-rational economic
policies India for so long followed. But it is nevertheless true
that as a consequence of the combination of the 'Left' atmosphere of the School and the Indian axiom that progress was
possible only through 'Left' policies, the alumni of the LSE—
mostly Indian, but non-Indian too—had an enormous impact
on our political, social and economic policies.

Among them was my distinguished contemporary Nicky
Kaldor whose theoretically perfect system of direct taxation
was modified by us in practice—as I warned him it would be—
into an absurd monstrosity which has had the most disastrous
effect on our economic development and in the dismantling of
which we have not yet fully succeeded. Nor was the economic
effect of V. K. Krishna Menon (senior to me but overlapping at
the edges) any better. I knew him well in my student days; he

was then as brilliant, as wild, as mordant, as dynamic, as
intolerant of opposition and as Left-wing in his thinking as he
was in later life. As a friend and confidant of Prime Minister
Nehru and as a Cabinet Minister, his political whack was far
too powerful for the somewhat more rational alumni of LSE to
withstand. Gaganvihari Mehta, J. J. Anjaria, R. S. Bhatt, Tony
Dias, Minoo Masani, P. S. Lokanathan and even Tarlok
Singh—all, except the first, my contemporaries—together with
divers other cogs in the administrative machine such as myself,
were swept aside as reactionary bourgeois stooges of the capitalist class!

My contact with my contemporaries was not very great.
Such as there was was with foreign students, principally Indian,
very little with English men or women. One of the disadvantages of a university located in a great city is that there is little
corporate life after academic hours. The University of London
Centre had not yet been built and there were virtually no
hostels—I gather there are many now—where students at the
School could live. All of us seemed to live miles away from the
School and from each other. There was a Students' Common
Room—as unkempt now as, I am sure, it was then, though it
did not strike me so!—but it was dead in the evenings. There
was the International Students' Club at 32 Russell Square but
an English student was rarely to be seen there. I used occasionally to go to the Indian Students' Hostel at 112 Gower Street
to play billiards or chess but there too there were no non-
Indians around.

The Indian student in England in the 'thirties was between
two worlds. A generation earlier, he had accepted British
rule in India as a law of nature. He had been thoroughly brain-
washed into believing that English civilization was the supreme
culmination of the long development of the human race; his
salvation lay in achieving as nearly as he could the manners
and the graces and the modes of thought and behaviour of his
masters. A generation later, the Indian student never gave a
thought to the possibility of his being inferior to anybody else;

he came to this country to study as other students go to other countries to widen their experience; he might have gone equally to America or the Soviet Union or Germany or France, as increasing numbers of them in fact do. Nor was there any point of conflict with English students, for Britain no longer ruled India.

By the 'thirties the British claim to superiority had been shattered. British rule in India was regarded as unfair, unjust, inequitable and without moral foundation. We all resented intensely its continuation against the repeatedly demonstrated will of the people; the resentment was at its height when the Civil Disobedience Movements under Gandhi's leadership had to be suppressed with considerable violence. True it is that, generally speaking, the English student of the 'thirties was not much enamoured of the imperial concept and the LSE, in particular, lent strong support for the concept of at least Dominion Status for India. But the psychological barrier in the Indian mind which the political situation created inhibited any approach on the Indian side, while the natural reserve of the English prevented any movement from theirs. By far the largest numbers of my non-Indian friends and acquaintances—and they were neither many nor intimate—were among English Jews. They were far from being insular and our common history of oppression formed a natural, though unspoken, bond between us. I recall with pleasure that Professor David Glass and Sir Samuel Goldman were among my distinguished contemporaries.

Nor was this of course the only reason. Throughout the world foreign students tend to form their own groups for they are all homeless and rootless and friendless. The natives have attachments and interests predating their contact with the newcomers. The LSE has always had a large number of foreign students; of this group, in my time, the Indians formed a large proportion. It was only natural that most of those with whom I spent my time were foreigners—Germans, Norwegians, Ethiopians, West Africans, Chinese. None of these friends of mine seem, however, to have made a mark in the world prominent enough for me to have heard of them, except Deressa of Ethiopia who rose to be Finance Minister of his country and its Ambassador to Washington, Ortona of Italy who occupied many high offices in the service of his country, and Perera, the Trotskyist Finance Minister of Sri Lanka.

Most of those, however, with whom I spent my time were Indians—some of whom of course subsequently became Pakistanis—both at the School and outside. Of them many (a list of names would be far too long) eventually made distinguished careers for themselves in the Civil and Diplomatic Services, in the Law and the Judiciary and in Politics (both in India and Pakistan), though not so many in business and industry. The only one who has made a name for himself in literature is Krishna Kripalani, the biographer of Tagore and Gandhi, with whom for more than one summer I walked home regularly through Hyde Park to South Kensington after the Library had closed at night, arguing violently all the way!

The School compensated for its geographical location in some measure by attempting to organize a corporate life of its own. There were many societies of all kinds: political, academic, cultural and regional, of which last the India Society was fairly active. I was not a joiner by nature and I do not recall being a member—at least an active one—of any, but I did follow the selective course of either gate-crashing or cadging an invitation—on payment I think!—to such meetings as promised to be interesting. The Union, of course, encompassed the whole School. In striking contrast to what it later became it never, during my time, even thought of developing an attitude of confrontation with the Management; the idea of student power had not yet been born. Compared to what it is today its sphere of responsibility was exceedingly small. Its public activities were limited to inviting distinguished public men to speak at it, or to holding debates in the Clare Market Parliament.

The playing fields of the LSE—on which no battles have been, or are likely to be, won—were then, as now, at Malden. This made it impossible, because of the sheer travel-time involved, for any but the most enthusiastic, the most intrepid and the most leisured to take advantage of them. (I was foolhardy enough in my first term to join the Rowing Club, but one autumn of wet and cold and soggy afternoons on the river at Hammersmith I found was as much as I could take!) Most of us therefore retreated to whatever amusement or relaxation was available within the School building or in its immediate geographical neighbourhood. There were very frequent lunch-time dances in the basement, from which the shy or the merely maladroit (such as myself) were naturally excluded. My own great favourite time-consumer was the badminton court, also in the basement, where the standard of play was high, and I eventually rose to be captain of the team. Another popular pastime was table-tennis, in the small room next to the Students' Common Room. There was also the possibility of tennis at the Lincoln's Inn Courts. If all else failed one went across Portugal Street to the Stoll Cinema, which must have made a goodly income from the students of the School! And I must not forget to mention the elegant Founders' Room, meant by its founders for quiet meditation or contemplation, but used by the students, more often than not, for quiet flirtation. But in spite of these distractions, not to mention those outside the School—the all-night sessions of bridge, the frequent visits to the theatre, the dining out with friends (I find I used to dine at restaurants much more as a student than I can afford to do now as a High Commissioner)—there prevailed at the School so great an atmosphere of learning that even the most unstudious (such as myself) could not fail to be affected by it.

There was such a galaxy of talent at the School at that time—to say nothing of visiting professors and guests either of the School or of some of its societies—that it was difficult to decide at what time which lecturer should have preference. There was the young and very handsome Lionel Robbins, tossing back his flowing mane of hair (to the delight of the ladies), lecturing to packed classes in the large lecture room on the ground floor. There was Hugh Dalton, lecturing on Public Finance, always punctuating his teaching with some anecdote of 'when I was at Foreign Office', which he had quit on the formation of the National Government in 1931. Lees-Smith, who lectured on Public Administration, had been Postmaster-General in the same Government but did not refer to his Ministerial experiences. Then there was Lauterpacht who lectured on International Law with such brilliance that the enthusiasm he evoked in me for this subject has not left me after more than forty years.

Hermann Finer had the distinction of being the only lecturer whose two enormous and very detailed volumes I read almost from end to end. I attended, too, Ivor Jennings on the Constitutional History of England, and plodded through Maitland's standard book on the subject. There was also that great authority, Eileen Power, who lectured on Economic History, a subject which, I now recognize, I could never really get to grips with owing to my immaturity. There was that unchallenged authority on the United States, Professor Brogan, who kindled my original interest in that country about which the British-Indian education of which I was a product had left me with the impression that it had ceased to exist in 1776. Whale and Benham on Banking and Currency were others who cast their pearls before me. And there were visitors, Professor von Hayek from Vienna, who was so much beyond me that I had to give him up fairly early, and Professor Viner from Chicago on International Trade whom I found fascinating. I never attended any of Professor Malinowski's lectures though I got to know him slightly through a student of his. Through him I remember being presented to Sir James Frazer, with the result that I spent an enormous amount of money buying *The Golden Bough*, a book which till today I have not had the opportunity to read. And once or twice I had the thrill of glimpsing the founders of the School, Sidney and Beatrice Webb, whose visits to it had by then become very few and far between.

The years passed pleasantly, fairly usefully and reasonably
actively, though the activity (as I have sometimes felt of late)
might have had better results if it had been less disjointed and
more concentrated. I got my degree in 1932 but hung around
the School for another year pursuing my dilettantist interests
before I moved on to Oxford. I have often wondered what it
was exactly that LSE did for me—and have not been able to
give a satisfactory answer. It was London—rather than LSE—
which forced me to a self-reliance to which I was unaccustomed.
It would probably have taken longer at the older universities,
with their more restrictive and protective rules, to break
through my sheltered cocoon. My earlier scientific training had
conditioned me to believe that two and two must always make
four; if they didn't there was something wrong somewhere. I
felt consequently much at home in the Law; it might have
been silly, archaic and complicated but it was at least logical.
I learnt the elements of Economics—which have stood me in
good stead; it was inexact but it nevertheless was a science.
But what was called Political Science, which was my special
subject and to which I did devote a great deal of study—based,
as I felt it was, on unproven assumptions of human nature and
wholly speculative theories of social organization—baffled me
to the very end. I do not believe that the human mind can
really comprehend or appreciate Political Theory till it has
been considerably matured through actual experience of the
practical world.

Apart from whatever academic knowledge was instilled into
me at the School, the totality of influences to which I was sub-
jected did have a very lasting and profound effect on my
personality in at least two respects. I never became a communist, in spite of the fashion of the times, for I rejected Marx's
oversimplifications and his solutions. But I did, and do, accept
the essential validity of the concept of historical materialism;
whence my effort in life has always been to change the economic pattern in the belief that social and political changes will
automatically follow. The second permanent result has been

my total opposition to hereditary privilege. I came from a country and an atmosphere highly stratified by caste and class to another which was perhaps even more so—and, surprisingly, still is. But the transformation in my thinking which would then at least not have taken place in Oxford or Cambridge (whence I believe my father's objection) was due to the LSE and was permanent. I was never converted to the idea of absolute equality, of which there were many proponents at the School, for I could not, and cannot, accept that there should be ceilings to human achievement, whether material or other. Equality of opportunity—exceedingly difficult to achieve no matter what the organization of society—is to me essential; insistence on the equality of attainment disastrous to the progress of civilization.

I said goodbye to Professor Laski when I left for India in 1934. I next met him in 1948 at a lunch given by Krishna Menon at India House. By then I had been a magistrate, a tax collector, a judge, the president of a cooperative bank, the president of a municipality, a central banker, an accountant— such were the opportunities for the Indian Civil Service!—and was at that time engaged in mismanaging India's external finances. I said to Professor Laski: 'I have a confession to make to you. In the fifteen years since I left you my political ideas have become the exact opposite of all you taught me.' I well remember his answer: 'I taught you no ideas. What I taught you was to think for yourself. If your own experiences in the School of Life have caused you, through your own independent thinking, to come to conclusions different from my own, I am happy. For I have succeeded in my aim: I have taught you how to think.' That, perhaps, is the greatest claim that a teacher or a school of learning can make for itself.

Aubrey Jones

Aubrey Jones was born in 1911 and attended the London School of Economics from 1929 to 1934. From 1937–39 and 1947–48 he was on the foreign and editorial staffs of The Times, during the intervening war period serving on the Army Intelligence Staff at the War Office and in the Mediterranean. He was MP for Birmingham, Hall Green from 1950–65; served as Parliamentary Private Secretary to the Minister of State for Economic Affairs in 1952 and to the Minister of Materials in 1953; and himself became Minister of Fuel and Power in December 1955. From 1957–59 he was Minister of Supply and from 1965–70 he was Chairman of the National Board for Prices and Incomes. He has been chairman and director of numerous companies and consultant on economic plans to Nigeria and Iran. His publications include The Pendulum of Politics (1946); Industrial Order (1950); The New Inflation; the politics of prices and incomes (1973).

It was chance rather than design which took me to the London School of Economics. My schoolboy ambition had been to become a barrister; names like Marshall-Hall, Birkett, gripped my imagination. My plans had been carefully laid. With the aid of a municipal scholarship, I was to go to the University College of Wales, Aberystwyth, which then had (and presumably still has) the reputation of having a good law school; thence I would go to an Inn still to be chosen. In that last summer vacation between school and university, the ambition was shattered. A local solicitor known to my family made it clear to me that my father could never support me in my first indigent years as a barrister. I had to use the scholarship to some other end and, in all probability, in some other place. But what and where?

I wrote to almost every university in the country, not really knowing what I wanted. My father wished me to become a nonconformist preacher, his own brother being one, and my mother a teacher, she herself having been one. I was determined to be neither. This state of ignorance made the courses offered by responding universities all the more unimaginative. Then, by accident, I came across the name—the 'London School of Economics.' I wrote away for the prospectus. When I had perused it, I decided immediately that this was where I had to go. It is difficult now to say precisely what allured me. Was it the subjects taught or was it the galaxy of teachers, many of whose names were then hitting the headlines as members of the first Labour Government—Sidney Webb, Lees-Smith, Dalton? Doubtless, it was a combination of both, but the names possibly were the more powerful component.

I applied, by post, for a place; was accepted; and then, by post, had to arrange accommodation. As far as I know, the School had at that time no hostel, but a list of agreeable lodgings was supplied. I chose from the list, chose further the landlady who replied most warmly, and on the scheduled day duly proceeded to London. I had never been there before, except for a day's visit, with others from my school, to the great Wembley Empire Exhibition in the 'twenties. At Paddington Station I was met by an aunt who worked as a cook in Hampstead. Together we went to the favoured lodging in Russell Square. The cordial landlady turned out to be repellent, the lodgings, though inhabited by a German post-graduate student of the School, to be absolutely foul, and without further ado I deserted. That evening my aunt and I tramped the streets of Bloomsbury, looking at other places on the list so kindly supplied by the School. We found one which was at any rate to serve me for a few nights.

That search for an abode was, however, to continue and consume much of my time during my first terms at the School, for I am afraid I have always been unduly sensitive to physical surroundings. The habitation finally chosen was an attic at 269 Gray's Inn Road. Only a short time ago, when I was by chance passing by, I saw the house being demolished. The bathroom was in the basement and in the warm summer nights, when the window was open, a stray cat would jump into my room and disturb my always fitful sleep. However, I was reasonably settled there.

The difficulties of my first year were compounded by illness. Accustomed to the air of Welsh hills, I could not acclimatize myself to the jaded atmosphere of London, and only the vacations spent at home would restore me to health. What was

worse, I knew I had chosen the wrong subject. Those were the
days of graduate unemployment and I was fearful of not finding
a job if and when I graduated. Accordingly, I chose an
apparently practical subject—Commerce. Some of the courses
were, however, dull and some of the teachers just plain boring.
With envy I looked upon those who had done more esoteric
things, such as the flamboyant, assured and handsome Graham
Hutton, and the less vivid, but still renowned Robert Fraser. I
was still overawed by the cosmopolitanism of the School, and
my main companion in those days of misery and humbleness
was a law student from North Wales, a little older than I. We
used to talk in the Common Room in Welsh, a language which,
I am ashamed to say, now lies in my memory beneath a pile of
other languages since accumulated.

It was only towards the end of my first year that I began to
find my feet. Then I decided to take the plunge. I suppose that
going to the School at all had been a bold enough move. Now
I decided on one that was even bolder. I decided for my second
year to switch courses and start all over again. I went for that
loftiest of subjects—Economics. I do not know why; the subject
appealed to me, even though the link between economics and
mathematics was already over the horizon and I had not been
schooled in advanced mathematics. Frederick Benham, whose
lectures had never excited me, helped me to effect the change.
And so, in rapid succession, I passed through the hands of a
line of tutors—Gilbert (now Professor Gilbert of Leeds University), Pakenham (now Longford, at the School for only a
short time pending his transit to the Research Department of
the Conservative Party), Durbin (alas, drowned), and Nicholas
Kaldor. Of them all, Kaldor was the most stimulating and the
most helpful.

One day, he did something unusual for a tutor. He said to
me with great assurance: 'You will have a first.' I was taken
aback with disbelief, but despite the disbelief the words gave
me a sense of confidence. Perhaps that is why he uttered them.
Perhaps he saw in me something of the foreigner in a strange

milieu which he himself had been, arriving as a Jew from
Budapest. Be that as it may, I owe to Nicholas Kaldor an
enormous debt of gratitude. And I only regret that, later than
it should have been, he finally obtained his Professorship, not at
the School, but at the hands of another university.

Nicholas Kaldor had at the School a Hungarian friend, who
in turn became my friend. He was, to the best of my recollection, an official of the Hungarian Ministry of Finance, and we
used to go for Sunday walks together in Kew Gardens. I cannot
remember his name, though I have undoubtedly kept at any
rate some of his letters; I have a tidy-minded wife who stows
away my papers in places that are almost inaccessible so that
I have difficulty in finding anything. I came across him again
in 1968, when I went to Budapest as the official guest of (I think
it was called) the Board for Prices and Materials. He came to
see me at the residence of the British Ambassador. He told me
how, on the morrow of the German invasion of Poland at the
beginning of the Second World War, there had appeared at the
portals of the Hungarian Ministry of Finance a refugee Pole,
who asked for the official who had spent some time in London.
'Ah,' said the porter, 'you must mean so-and-so' (i.e., my
friend). The Pole too had been a student at the School. Thus
did the School bind together people of diverse origins.

My Hungarian friend had apparently risen to the position
of Permanent Secretary of the Ministry only to be dismissed on
his refusal to sign up as a member of the Party. On the occasion
of my seeing him, he was living in his native village, seemingly
in poverty-stricken circumstances. On that account he refused
all invitations by the Ambassador to receptions. He will remain
one of the unsung of the School, who none the less derived
something from the School and from whom others of the School
derived a great deal.

My new-found confidence and my enthusiasm for economics
prompted me to be one of the first in the mornings to wait
outside the locked library doors. By virtue of this punctuality, I
acquired a desk which was permanently mine. It was up in the

gallery, with an inspired view of the metal fire escape, stained with pigeon droppings. A rose-cheeked girl doing social administration used sometimes to come and sit alongside me, invariably belatedly; but I was too absorbed in economics to be really interested. The occupant of the table behind mine was a post-graduate student named Neumann, doing research into the British coal industry. With a name like that he could have come from anywhere and gone anywhere. Others with their permanent niches in the library were Ursula Hicks (what was her maiden name?), Abba Lerner, whom I last saw in the late 'sixties in San Francisco, and, I believe, Samuel Goldman. They dwelt on the ground floor, and were senior to me. Why somehow does one remember seniors more clearly than juniors? Occasionally, I would leave the main library for the statistical library, to look up something special and incidentally to observe the grace of the late Honor Croome. The School's contribution to the London and Cambridge Economic Survey, then, I suppose, in its infancy, was being compiled there.

Long hours in the library were interrupted by the odd visit to the political meeting. I went to meetings organized by all three parties. Those of the Labour Party were the liveliest and the best attended. Those of the Conservative Party were the dullest and the attendance was sparse. Liberal audiences were equally thin. It was to the Liberal Party, however, that I briefly subscribed; I ended my association after having heard a speech by Sir Archibald Sinclair. By far the keenest political interest was evoked by Marxism. Hitler had appeared and his appearance had given a fillip to Left-wing thinking. Simultaneously, Sidney Hook had just published his condensation of Marx; and this helped to make that massive and obscure writer a little more intelligible. Most Common Room conversations were taken up with Marxism, and I was a participant. This particular flirtation ended, however, when I was invited to take part in a demonstration through Hyde Park. My non-conformist upbringing shrank from such an act of ostentation.

While I was still flirting, I went to an exposition on Marx

given by John Strachey. He was not of the School but came to the School. Later, we became friends in the House of Commons. He would not remember me, sitting quietly and obscurely at the back of the hall, and I never sought to remind him. Another who was not of the School but came to it, though not to a political meeting—to some kind of financial seminar, I think— was Balogh. To me he was a figure of awe, being no less than an adviser to the Bank of England. Him too I came to know later, and to feel that he was a far too little appreciated person.

Political meetings were not, of course, the main interruption to those long hours in the library. The principal cause of intrusion was attendance at seminars and lectures. On my peregrinations back and forth I sometimes caught glimpses of the Great—the Director, the bird-like Beveridge, and the Secretary, the over-powering Mrs Mair. Was she, I wonder, a Pauline? I never had directly to do with her. In so far as I had an administrative problem or wished to change from this to that, I went to the ever kind and ever helpful Miss Evans. How the School would have run without her I do not know.

For some strange reason one never had a tutor after the first year. Instead, one went to seminars. I attended seminars guided by John Hicks. He would puff musingly away at his pipe while the paper of the day was being presented. Hicks was cool and detached, and did not share easily in the en- thusiasms of the School, or for that matter in enthusiasms from any other quarter. He committed the heresy of being an early convert to Keynesianism, then abhorred by the School. It was his very detachment which was so attractive about Hicks. On one occasion, after I had given a paper on some aspect of international trade, he was particularly kind to me. Later he took me to his flat and gave me my first ever sip of whisky. Was it for this that my temperate father had slaved to help send me to the university?

Attendance at seminars I, at any rate, regarded as obligatory, though whether it was so or not I do not know. Attendance at lectures I regarded more casually, partly because there used to be circulated an attendance sheet, which one might or might not sign, depending upon whether or not it reached one. There were lectures which did not form part of the course, though one would have liked to go had time allowed. I would like to have heard Professor Bowley on Statistics; instead I learned my statistics from Dr Rhodes. I would like to have heard on Sociology T. H. Marshall, whom I used to see emerging from the depths of the School swinging a badminton racquet. And certainly I would like to have heard on Economic History Professor Tawney, accounts of whom I used to hear from a friend reading that subject. However, I read Tawney's book on Equality and was entranced by the style. I tried to read the book again the other day and failed; the style put me off. Why is it that one changes in some respects and not in others?

Despite the casualness which I attached to lectures there were not many that I deliberately missed. However, I confess to having eschewed those on Public Finance given by Dalton. I had already read his book and went to the first lecture of his course. I never went again.

The lectures which most affected me were those of Robbins, Hayek, Laski and Postan. Robbins, long of hair and sonorous of phrase, had passion and his thought could be grasped without much difficulty. Both passion and thought infected me. I went home to an unemployed father and argued vehemently with him that the only cure for unemployment was a reduction in wages. Conscience and intellect, if they can be separated, both prick me now. In one particular peroration Robbins spoke of the generation lost in the First World War and insisted that such a calamity must never recur. We were all intensely moved. Spontaneously, we rose to our feet and gave him a standing ovation. It is the only such occasion that I can recall.

Hayek came to London straight from Vienna, en route, it subsequently turned out, for Chicago. He wore a perpetually benevolent smile, a trait which did not belie his nature. But

his accent in English was thick and his thought appeared
tangled. One had to sit near the front in order to try and
follow. I clearly remember a declamation against housing
subsidies in the Socialist Austria of post-1918. But I would be
hard put to it now, without re-reading the books, lucidly to
describe Hayek's standpoint in the controversy with Keynes.
He undoubtedly became the leader of the LSE camp in the
war of words with Cambridge.

As a lecturer Laski was by far the most fascinating and as a
human being he had probably the softest heart. He would
never stand for his lectures; he always sat, twiddling his thumbs
and speaking without notes. The discourse would be inter-
larded with anecdotes of the great—Roosevelt, Lloyd George,
even Ramsay MacDonald (though he was not considered
great). The hero in every episode of man's epic struggle for
freedom was invariably Frankfurter, later of the United States
Supreme Court. It was all great stuff. No wonder the lecture
room was crowded and Laski's influence spread far beyond the
shores of the British Isles. But when I got back to the library
and sat down to write up my notes, I was dimly conscious
of a flaw in the argument; I could never quite place it, but
instinct told me that somewhere there was a gap.

Not that it mattered, for Laski was also a host. He was, to
the best of my knowledge, the only teacher who gave tea
parties to students. I used to repair, every Sunday afternoon,
to the house near Addison Bridge and gaze awe-struck at the
book-lined walls. Mrs Laski once pinned me in a corner and
urged on me the need for contraception. I can think of no
reason why she should have me particularly in mind and I can
only imagine that she was talking in general; it seemed an odd
subject for conversation over Sunday afternoon tea, but I
suppose the young have to be moulded while they are young.
Floating around there was also Miss Laski; contraception
suggests that there could have only been one. Both to the delight
and the distress of her father she was bad at economics; a
friend of mine, Owen Williams, who was later to enter the

Civil Service, was asked to coach her; how they got on together I do not know.

Laski's kindness was not confined to tea parties, despite mordant articles about living politicians which appeared every week in the then *Daily Herald*. When, towards the end of my days at the School, I inflicted fresh difficulties upon myself, his door was invariably open to me and he would give me what advice he could. He once said to a friend of mine that I was a very practical chap; I still ask myself if he was right. The last time I ever saw Laski was a year or two after I had left the School; he was seated all alone on the empty terrace of a café in the Boulevard Saint Michel, immersed in a book; I wondered whether or not I should go up to him, but I refrained. I have since regretted my hesitancy, for around a decade or so after my departure from the School we fought the first post-war General Election from opposing sides of the political battle-field; I dislike the simile, but it is conventionally used, so why not use it? As a result of that election he acquired the image of something evil incarnate. The image does not square with the Laski whom I had known either in lectures or over tea.

The lecturer, however, who left the most lasting impression on me was Postan, lecturing in Economic History. His name is no longer associated with the School, but to my mind, then and still, his lectures showed a greater depth of thought than those of any other teacher. He described events, not as isolated phenomena, but in their patterns, moving, despite the randomness of things human, in a course as pre-ordained as any in the heavens. This was not a thought which I easily accepted. Indeed in the examination paper on Economic History which I had to do in my finals, I challenged it. Postan, however, does not seem to have minded. When the examination results came out he invited me to his room, though we had never before spoken tête-à-tête. It was one of the earlier rooms on the eastern side of Houghton Street as distinct from the original building on the western side. He told me that I had done a better paper than any of the historians and that I had made a mistake in reading Economics; I should have read History. It was a shrewd comment and in long retrospect I know that he was right. I have never since seen Postan, much though I have wished to.

Aside from the lectures given by internal teachers, there were those given by the visitor; attendance at these was clearly optional. The visitor whom I most vividly recall was Jacob Viner, of Chicago; there seems to have been a long-standing fraternal bond between the School and Chicago. The subject of his lectures, given in the theatre off the main foyer which was then as it still is, was International Trade. What his message was I do not remember. There floats through my memory only the figure—an enormous head and brow, almost too large for the body, surmounted by a mane of black hair. I was very sensitive to features in those days. There was one other occasion in the theatre which I shall never forget. The speaker may possibly have been Hayek. But it was not the speaker or what he said that mattered. What mattered was the fact that I sat near Keynes. I had already heard Keynes talk at a Sunday evening lecture of the Fabian Society; and I had instantly become a hero-worshipper. I did not then know what I now know—namely, that because of a difference of view a temporary estrangement had arisen between Keynes and Professor D. H. Robertson. Inevitably, therefore Robertson was invited to the School. But his lectures were never as droll as his book on Money, each chapter prefaced with an exquisite extract from *Alice in Wonderland*.

To know economics then one had to know German. And to learn German one had to traipse one's way, dodging the traffic, to the ghastly gloom of King's College. There I was severely ticked off for not being able to pronounce properly the word 'Haus'. With the smattering of German thus gleaned, I tried to plough my way through von Mises and Böhm-Bawerk. I doubt whether I did it very successfully.

After much reading and less listening one had to face the fateful week of the final examinations. The weather was hot;

the cats through the attic window were more intrusive than usual; and sleep, fitful at best, was fugitive. The papers on economics arose straight from Robbins's *The Nature and Significance of Economic Science*, and I duly articulated the Faith. The paper on statistics could not by definition give rise to controversy. The papers on political science and economic history were, however, challenging, and, perversely, I took up the challenge. Lastly, there was a general essay to write. I believe I wrote about historiography, thereby betraying sub-consciously the influence of Postan. I was exhausted and depressed, and in my eyes had performed abominably.

With the close of the examinations term effectively ended, and my entitlement to scholarship funds ceased; I had to find a job. On the notice-board in the den of the Appointments Adviser there appeared an advertisement to the effect that a secretary-cum-research assistant was required by the Parliamentary Private Secretary to Sir John Simon, then Foreign Secretary. Several of us trooped down to the House of Commons to be interviewed. I was asked for my views on the likely price of silver. It was not clear to me then, nor is it now, what relevance the question had to the depression of the 'thirties. However, I made a prediction and, much to my surprise, was given the job.

For the several weeks that it takes examiners to mark examination papers—and they invariably seem to be very slow about it—I hovered round the outskirts of the famous. There had never been a telephone in my own home and at the School I had made but scant use of the instrument. Now I had to use it perpetually, frightened at every peal and being very ham-fisted. I also had to learn to use a typewriter, again an exasperating novelty. The World Economic Conference was on at the Geological Museum in Kensington. I used to go there nearly every day. It was my first experience of these international jamborees. Titbits of gossip pass from mouth to mouth, wisps of rumour float mysteriously through the air, but few retain a grasp of the main substance. The Conference

ended in failure. It seemed such a disaster at the time. Now it
does not seem to have mattered. Germany lifted herself out of
depression first by public works, which I had been taught to
abhor—fancy digging holes in the ground in order to fill them
up again!—and then by rearmament. In Britain and in the
United States recovery took place later through rearmament
alone—guns being made to destroy, the destruction then
necessitating reconstruction; another way, in short, of making
holes in the ground to fill them up again.

While I was still plodding away at the typewriter and
nervously handling the telephone, I received a call one day
from Robbins. Would I go and see him in his room? I do not
think I had ever before been face to face with Robbins; I had
revered him only from afar. He told me that I had obtained
the best First of the year, and indeed the best for several years,
though how that comparison could be made was not quite
clear to me. He added: 'You seem very modest about it.' I was
just dumbfounded with disbelief. My incredulity was overcome
only when I finally saw it all on paper. I was entitled to a
prize—the Gladstone—consisting of books of my choosing to a
value which I can no longer remember. The choice was
influenced in part by Laski, in part by Hayek; it thus consisted
of an odd combination of books by French rationalist thinkers
and books by economists of the Austrian school. I was also
entitled to a post-graduate scholarship which, after discussion
with Robbins, I decided to take up. Thereupon, I abandoned
my post by the typewriter and the telephone, and repaired to
Wales, where for the rest of the summer I avidly read Henry
James on the summit of the Brecon Beacons.

I returned from the Welsh mountains wearing a robustness
which ill became the asceticism appropriate to an ardent
researcher. However, I set about my research. It was on some
aspect of savings and investment; the theme was inspired by
Hayek, under whose tutelage I was. There was the occasional
distraction, such as the reviewing of a book for the School's
magazine, the *Clare Market Review*, the arrogance of youth

tempting me to make the review as caustic as possible. In the main, however, I concentrated on my research; the more I concentrated, the unhappier I became. I wanted to spread my wings, perhaps geographically, certainly intellectually. Economics was the study of a particular kind of social behaviour; how could one understand that behaviour without looking at society as a whole? How could one talk about investment without the study of Marx, and how could one properly understand Marx without the study of Hegel? What was the fundamental purpose of econometrics, or the study of the statistical relationship between one variable and another, when one was not quite sure which was cause and which was effect, and one certainly did not know how the relationship might change as psychology changed with changing social institutions? In short, I became plagued with doubts and felt I was digging myself deeper and deeper into a narrow groove. Accordingly, I applied for the diversion of my scholarship funds to a wider purpose.

Permission had to be obtained from on high. And so, one day, I proceeded aloft, to a sanctum where I had never been before. I am still not clear where exactly it was; I think it may have been what is now the Senior Common Room. I was nervous and my memory, possibly affected by living subsequently in the Orient, is befuddled. I retain the impression of having entered a Sultan's petitioning chamber; the Sultan (Beveridge) sat in the centre, flanked on either side by his advisers, myself deferentially distant. There was a vague pinkness about it all; it may have been the decor; or it may have been the gowns, worn unusually to impress. It was the Sultan in the main who asked the questions. I doubt whether he understood, or could have understood, what was really happening to me. In due course the conclave's judgement was communicated to me; I was turned down.

That humble petition was, however, a portent of things to come. The doubts which led to it have strengthened with the passage of the years. I question now whether the School, or indeed any other university, with each faculty and sub-faculty a mini-empire unto itself, can mount the multi-disciplinary approach required for the solution of many-sided contemporary problems.

The refusal was bound to force me back to the original subject of research or make me all the more determined to break away. The latter, of course, was the inevitable result. At this time of trouble nobody was more helpful than Robbins. He outlined a career for me and indeed almost started me on it. I was to become an economic and financial journalist. A job was arranged with a reputable newspaper. But even then there were take-overs, and the newspaper in question disappeared into the maw of another, to become, of its kind, pre-eminent. I was left dangling in uncertainty as to whether my job was still on or not. In this state of incertitude the International Labour Office in Geneva combed through British universities for a statistician to do a six-month job. Once again Robbins helped. I was chosen.

In going to the School at all I had voyaged some distance from my moorings in Wales. Now I was to voyage further, both geographically and intellectually. The night train journey to Geneva was my first trip to the European Continent. I fell in love with life on the European mainland. And, my six-month job up, I forsook economics and statistics for political journalism and, later, politics. I had cast myself away from the School and, from a combination of shame and shyness, did not re-enter it until, many years later, I became one of the first batch of Honorary Fellows, a distinction now shared by many others. How strange it was, on that night of re-entry, to find myself remembered. I was deeply touched.

The film, however, has run on too fast, and I have to roll it back. When I left the School, I doubt whether my views of the world differed substantially from those which I had been taught. In economics I suppose I was still basically 'laissez–faireist', and in politics and history doubts had certainly begun to appear about the validity of that which I had been told, but not so overwhelmingly as to destroy the teaching. My further voyaging, however, provoked a profound change of view, in all fields.

I was subsequently rash enough to expound these newer views in a book. Many years later I was asked by a teacher at the School: 'What in that book did you write that was derogatory to the School?' I could not, off-hand, answer the question. Certainly I could not bear to re-read something which I had written in my youth; I would probably have laughed at the whole thing. I could only reply that I could not consciously have tried to decry the School; my years there were among the happiest of my life, equalled perhaps by two such spells at a later date. Nor would it be in my nature to decry; I am too polite. I can imagine only that the views expressed exposed me to the charge of apostasy—of professing beliefs different from those first inculcated. This thought has profoundly distressed me. It has led me to reflect that the most illiberal could possibly be the most professedly liberal. And further, if a former student may so speak to teachers, that the aim of the teacher should not be to impress on the mind a form thereafter to be regarded as permanent; the aim rather should be to encourage the mind to evolve, even though the 'ultimate' shape, assuming that there is an 'ultimate', may differ considerably from that initially imprinted. For all these misgivings I recognize that I owe to the School an enormous debt which I have repaid inadequately, and which I owe it to my conscience to repay to the full.

Norman MacKenzie

Norman MacKenzie was a student at the London School of Economics from 1939–43. His wife Jeanne Sampson was a contemporary at the School. For twenty years he was assistant editor of the New Statesman, *then in 1962 he went to the University of Sussex and became Director of its School of Education. The MacKenzies have jointly written a biography of H. G. Wells and a study of the early Fabians. Among Norman MacKenzie's other books are* Women in Australia, Dreams and Dreaming, Secret Societies, The Letters of Sidney and Beatrice Webb, *and* Open Learning. *He was a Labour candidate in the General Elections of 1951 and 1955.*

J walked into the School for the first time on a spring afternoon in 1939. Upstairs, ranged round a large table and darkly silhouetted against the window, sat a formidable board conducting the oral examinations for the Leverhulme scholarships. The Director, Alexander Carr-Saunders—donnish but sympathetic—presided: flanking him were Lionel Robbins, T. H. Marshall, Lance Beales, F. A. von Hayek, Morris Ginsberg, Harold Laski and some others I have forgotten. To me they were names from the spines of books. Climbing up Sidney Webb's scholarship ladder from his old LCC constituency of Deptford I had never met an author or an academic, and I was more apprehensive than hopeful. Fortunately they gave me an easy time, for while I waited deferentially, school cap in hand, I had already been unnerved. Through the door of the committee-room I heard the rolling boom of Kurt Lewenhak, the candidate who preceded me, punctuated by laughter from the board. I knew I could not match such relaxed confidence, for too much depended on the interview. My inability to cope with Latin meant, at that time, that it must be London University or nowhere. The fact that I needed a scholarship meant that I must succeed. In any case, an obsession with politics had convinced me that LSE was the only place I wished to go.

I have a hunch that I coasted home on the coat-tails of

Lewenhak's humour, for I interviewed badly. Naive, self-
conscious and anxious, I struggled to make an impression. My
only distinct recollection is of Lionel Robbins reaching for
some point of contact and asking me if I read 'the reviews'.
Never having heard the phrase used to describe the weekly
papers I snatched at the chance to treat the board to a garbled
summary of a review I had read in the latest issue of the
Economist. 'Most interesting,' said Carr-Saunders in a gentle
dismissive way, glancing along the board. When next morning
a letter came on LSE stationery, I was so sure I was sunk that I
could not open it at once, and scarcely believed the offer to
start at Clare Market in October.

In fact I never entered the building as a student. Within
six months it was occupied, first by the Ministry of Economic
Warfare and then by the Air Ministry. In the course of that
summer, as war approached, plans were made to move the
School away from London. Cambridge was to offer it hospital-
ity, providing lecture theatres, library and sports facilities,
offices and lodgings. Peterhouse, the host college, turned over
its New Court (renamed The Hostel) to the School's administration. Grove Lodge, elegant but cosy and facing Addenbrooke's
Hospital across its pleasant garden, became an all-purpose
centre for the life of the School. Bedrooms were converted into
seminar-rooms. One was to house the cultural library which
Charlotte Shaw donated to widen the narrow minds of social
scientists. There was a lending-library tucked into a ground
floor which also contained a small canteen, a common room, a
Union office and the never-empty room for table-tennis.
Several hundred students were to make do with less space
than a students' union would today expect for its offices. And
space was only one of the problems that faced the School when,
at the beginning of September, it left London for the duration.
By scurrying and ingenuity the problems were overcome so
well that when we arrived on 2 October it seemed that LSE
had been a going concern on Trumpington Street for years.

For those who had known the School in London the change

was dramatic. It was a change of scale as well as place. In Houghton Street there had been 90 staff and 3,000 students, half of them part-time. Nine professors and 35 lecturers, some 500 undergraduates and a small group of research students turned up in Cambridge. (As the war went on the staff slowly dwindled but the student numbers, to everyone's surprise, actually increased: the post-war swing to the social sciences had already begun.) It was also a change in character. The part-timers had gone, though until the bombs came the School maintained a reduced programme for them at Canterbury Hall. In Clare Market there had been three men students for every woman; in Cambridge at first the numbers were even. Delays in call-up enabled school-leavers to spend a year and sometimes two at the School, returning to complete after demobilization, but by the middle of the war there were two women for every man. There were academic adjustments, too. If the School was to maintain anything like a full syllabus, since its staff was depleted by departures to Government departments and other war work, it had to dovetail with Cambridge faculties. It was a mutually beneficial arrangement. LSE students found themselves listening to A. C. Pigou, C. R. Fay and Joan Robinson; Cambridge students could cram the Mill Lane lecture-theatres to hear Harold Laski, R. H. Tawney, Nicky Kaldor, Hayek and Morris Ginsberg—the latter exposing them to the illicit subject of Sociology like a bootlegger suddenly licensed to sell gin in public. Regulations and curriculum were gently bent to profit from this unexpected partnership.

The decisive change, however, was the conversion of the School from a co-educational college of commuters to a residential community. This was not only a novelty for LSE, which marks off the students who only knew the school in wartime from the generations before and after who knew only Clare Market. It was a startling innovation for Cambridge. It was a university which had only grudgingly accepted women, suitably segregated and chaperoned, and for long awarded merely courtesy degrees. And it was thirty years after LSE had demonstrated that co-education was possible on the banks of the Cam that the Cambridge colleges began to open their gates on equal terms. There were, doubtless, grumbles over the common-room port about this wartime sacrifice. I am told that the proctors sighed as the pubs and blacked-out streets filled with gownless young men and women who were not 'members of this University'—and provided a camouflage for those who were. Yet, whatever secret stresses there may have been, Cambridge accepted its temporary symbiosis with the School with remarkable grace and generosity. For the students of the School—as for those from Queen Mary and Bedford colleges who had been similarly accommodated—the translation worked like a dream.

For me, coming fresh to the School in the first weeks of war, it also felt like a dream. I had planned to live at home and make my daily tram ride up the Queen's Road to Kingsway; instead, I found myself temporarily billeted in a manor house outside Cambridge, cycling in through the autumn mist to King's Parade. I was going to be a student, but first of all I was an evacuee, as plainly as if I had arrived like a schoolchild with a label and gas-mask strung round my neck. Britain, in those weeks, was playing a great game of general post which jumbled up people and moved them across all kinds of social frontiers. The effect was confusing, stressful and sometimes salutary: as much as any other aspect of the war it gave the frame of the class-system a shake from which it never recovered. Just as the School and Cambridge had to come to terms, so I struggled to bridge the gap between high tea and candlelit dinner. I think my hosts, though graciously tolerant, found it as hard to take the shelf of Left Book Club volumes in my bedroom as I—stiff with hot-house socialism—did to relax among the smart young people who filled the house at week-ends and gossiped nicknames and yachting and horses. It was not easy for the Two Nations to talk to each other.

Grove Lodge was another matter. We were all evacuees.

We came from similar backgrounds, talked with much the same accents, discovered common interests. And, uprooted and crowded together, we found it easy to make friends. The atmosphere was like that on a liner at the start of a long voyage or, perhaps, like a summer school. The enthusiasts started up their clubs: newcomers signed up on the lists on Grove Lodge lobby with equal alacrity and with little discrimination. I recall the frisson in the first meeting of the Rugby club when Renate Kucynski turned up and claimed that at LSE anyone could join anything. You could take your pick between Basil Bonner's Rationalists, Gwilym Morgan's Student Christian Movement, the Socialist Society, the Majlis, music, amateur dramatics, half-a-dozen sports or intellectual pastimes. From the beginning of the war to the end that Grove Lodge lobby was decorated with signs and slogans like a float in a May Day parade; and, like a parade, you could scarcely push your way through without being sold or given homiletic literature. Having served my time in this little market-place of ideas I am certain that my contemporaries were the most insatiable consumers of anything in print—or even in barely legible duplication—that I have ever known.

In the first months of the war this buzz of activity helped the School to find its own identity in unfamiliar surroundings. It was the student counterpart of its academic individuality, providing a secure base for the complex relationships which soon developed with Cambridge as students began to plug in to the network of undergraduate societies just as the staff came to share their teaching with Cambridge colleagues. The Cambridge life-style soon rubbed off on us; it is harder to say what rubbed off LSE on to Cambridge. From the outset dances were common ground; so were the flickering film shows in the basement off Petty Cury where the Cambridge University Socialist Club ran *We from Kronstadt*, *The Last Days of St Petersburg* and Fritz Kortner's endless *Warning Shadows*. But LSE rowed, played rugger, hockey and squash with Cambridge teams, and philosophers, madrigal singers and logicians soon found fellow-spirits. You could get into anything except the Union Society, the Pitt Club and the Apostles. There was all Cambridge as a context. Grove Lodge had its own outposts at Tulliver's for coffee and tea, at the Little Rose for beer; in a Cambridge where women were still in minority the more genteel members of the Social Work course got taken up and out to the Copper Kettle, the Whim, Matthew's and KP or Toni's for a posh meal. The Blue Barn, perched above the Red commune of Round Church Street, was cheap Chinese for the evening out, with *Duck Soup* or *Dr Mabuse* at the Cosmo to top off the chop suey. Even before the airmen and later the Americans began to crowd in at nights the dark streets seemed full of people going somewhere, for there was always somewhere to go—big meetings at the Dorothy, or the Co-op Hall, little meetings in Round Church Hall, or college JCRs, or in someone's room, plays at the Arts or the ADC, dancing out at the Rex. In winter there were walks to Grantchester, in summer the Backs and punts on the river; and every day there was the visual reward of Cambridge itself as one cycled to the University Library, the Marshall or the Seeley or simply wandered up to browse in Heffer's or Bowes and Bowes.

This description makes it sound like a student utopia. So it was. Despite the war—or because of it?—there was a zestful busyness about those first months quite unlike anything I had known. Part of that excitement was simply the effect of growing up and discovering a world so different from a boys' grammar-school on the genteel fringe of London's tramland. Part of it was undoubtedly the intensity and range of friendships. The camaraderie of Grove Lodge did something to account for the fact that one made friends so easily; so did the heightening impact of war and evacuation—the latter may explain why so many of us seem to have married fellow-students and why friendships then formed have survived the years. It was also a matter of variety. Before I arrived at Grove Lodge I think I had met no more than half-a-dozen Europeans. By the end of my first term I had become fast friends with an Iraqi, an

Iranian, a Siamese and a Turk, and I had soon added German and Austrian refugees, Indians, East Africans, a Burmese and an Australian. The School had always attracted overseas students and enough of them were marooned by the war to provide a vicarious introduction to Europe, the Commonwealth and a scattering of countries in between. Later, too, came a group of Polish officers (a strain on the political susceptibilities of the Left) and Czechs (politically more congenial, but too many of them later victims of the Cold War purges). The Union meetings in the OCR at Trinity became a microcosm of the future United Nations.

For the first two terms there was not much to make one uneasy at so much privileged pleasure. The Polish war was over. The Russian army ground away at Finland through the winter. The British and French sat out the 'phoney war' along the Belgian and German frontiers. But in Cambridge, as in the rest of the country, life went on much as usual apart from such minor inconveniences as the blackout and the beginning of rationing. True, the call-up was creeping on, and in the meantime there were afternoons at the Senior Training Corps or the University Air Squadron. But the war was a long way off in reality.

Things changed in May: France was falling as we sat examinations in the Senate House. In June, a casual Dornier bombed Vicarage Terrace into something of a tourist attraction. It was only when I arrived at Liverpool Street station at the beginning of the summer vacation and passed a line of dirty and exhausted survivors from Dunkirk that the headlines became real: Grove Lodge had indeed been a cosy retreat from the world which had begun to bang away beyond its gate.

The longer one stayed at Cambridge the stronger this sense of opting out of events became—I think most of us felt an embarrassing contrast between our luck and the tribulations of others. After all, as the saying went, there was a war on. Though wartime pressures undoubtedly intensified that feeling I do not now believe it was peculiar to those years. Many students feel ambivalent about their temporarily privileged status. For three years they live in a comfortable and stimulating suspense from normal obligations. They have admirable facilities for leisure as well as interesting work. No longer adolescents, they are still dependents. Not quite adult, they are protected from responsibility. It is a curious interregnum whose paradoxes confuse the borderline of fantasy and fact.

It is this confusion, I think, which explains the special character of student politics and the persistence of a similar posture from one generation of Left-wingers to another, whether the current slogan is to send Arms to Spain, Open the Second Front, Ban the Bomb, Stop the War in Vietnam or Back the Rent Strike. I have no doubt that our predecessors felt just as strongly about Spain as we did about Nazi Germany and our successors did about CND, just as earnest and emotional, just as frustrated in the conviction that the world must be set to rights, and quickly. It is a matter of posture, though it seems to be a matter of issues: the latter are merely the vehicles for an impulse which stems from much deeper causes. It is because students are privileged that they campaign against privilege, because they are in fact powerless that they have fantasies of omnipotence. Organization and agitation provide a release for guilt, becoming almost ends in themselves. It is this that makes student groups so vulnerable to changes in political fashion, substituting one urgent cause for another. It also does something to explain why middle-class students are more prone to radical extremes than those from working-class backgrounds.

I have thought a good deal about this problem because the war years at Cambridge provided such a clear demonstration of the process. To put it simply, at the beginning the prevailing political mood was one of dubiety about the war, if not of overt opposition. Two years later, the reverse was true. That, in itself, is not remarkable. What is remarkable that these opposite policies were advanced with equal fervour, by the same people, by the same means, through the same organizations. The nearest analogy I can find is that of a repertory company switching from *The Murder of Maria Marten in the Red Barn* to *Hamlet* and finding its audience equally enthusiastic.

The leading actors in this case, of course, were members of the Communist Party (though my argument would apply today to the International Socialists or similar groups of radical activists). As one who joined the CP in the first phase and carried over into the second I can speak from first-hand knowledge of the process I am describing. Since it was one that did much to colour LSE in the war years it is worth pursuing a little further.

First of all, much nonsense has been talked about the School as a hotbed of communism. It was never true in any degree of the staff, though wild men of the Right treated Harold Laski as a convenient Aunt Sally: I doubt whether a majority of the faculty even voted for the Labour Party, and there were notable Conservatives and Liberals amongst them. And communists were never more than a small minority of the students. At its wartime peak the CP group in the school did not reach ten per cent of the total student numbers and very few of its recruits were ever—in the party's jargon—really 'Bolshevized'. I can only think of two who survived to become lifelong members.

Secondly, it was not so much the policy of the CP that attracted members and influenced a much larger number of students as, so to speak, its dramatic personality. Up to September 1939 the Communist Party was the protagonist of the Popular Front. From 1939 to 1941 it played a different role. It hesitated to come out unambiguously against the war effort. Off-stage it encouraged its members to study Volume V of Lenin's selected works and other texts on revolutionary defeatism; on-stage it went through the motions of the People's Convention. (The gestures of this 'front' organization, combining nods towards democracy and winks towards its Stalinist prompters, were confusing at the time and easily forgotten thereafter.) On 22 June 1941 the repertoire was changed again.

The People's Convention was suddenly dropped and the communists found themselves playing 'Everything for the Second Front' to packed audiences in the best theatres. What did not vary was the ability of the Communist Party machine to meet the need to organize and agitate.

It had, of course, competitors and critics. Until Stalin swung the communists back behind the war there were vocal social-democrats, both staff and students, who did their best to ridicule the ease with which the party line switched from anti-fascism to anti-war. There were some arcane varieties of Trotskyist who were free-lance snipers at Stalin and all his works. There were a few strong-minded individualists who reacted instinctively against machines and manipulation. Judged by subsequent events they had the better argument, though at the time they seemed to have the worst of it. Fabian tracts were prosaic and lacked the intellectual certainties of cheap Marxist texts from Lawrence and Wishart. Official Labour policy was unexciting and, in the wartime party truce, there was not much space for socialist rhetoric or knockabout propaganda against Toryism. The Trotskyists seemed perverse deviants. And the individualists were mostly reduced to comic turns at Union meetings. None of these could effectively challenge the organizational drive of the CP. Though small in membership it could ensure a steady flow of the *Daily Worker, World News and Views* and *Labour Monthly*, speakers, resolutions, Soviet films and candidates for Union and other elections. It was also backed by a Cambridge organization which had peaked during the Spanish civil war, providing its own martyrs in John Cornford and David Guest. In MacLaurin's bookshop and its network in the colleges it still retained a considerable potential for propaganda.

Despite its change in policy the Communist Party continued to profit from the campaign against Chamberlain—it never was more right—the glamour of the International Brigade and the reputation of the Soviet Union as the first socialist state. By one of those curious time-lags one often finds in politics it succeeded in drawing on the credit of the anti-fascist 'thirties while supporting the Moscow line against the war: party discipline and tortuous dialectics helped to justify the partition of Poland and the campaign against Finland. It was also—and this helped in a School with so many overseas students and much distaste for the Empire—anti-imperialist. Above all it talked indefatigably about socialist theory. Possessing such assets it was bound to set the political tone. Even those who opposed it found themselves arguing on its premises; and in its anti-war phase it managed to profit from an air of martyrdom and what now seems a comic atmosphere of conspiracy.

Everyone knew where it met, but its members carefully chose devious routes to meetings as if followed by the Gestapo. Everyone knew that it was run from three houses in the warren of Round Church Street, an agreeable commune where members no longer *in statu pupillari* could use the beds in daytime in exchange for duplicating propaganda bulletins all night, but it had no formal existence. Everyone knew, too, who were the party candidates for office in the Socialist Society or the Union, but they never ran under a party label. There was a great deal of play-acting at being revolutionaries—and that was also a source of fascination. It was not surprising that, whatever the vagaries of the party line, the communists could make all the running.

It is true that I was one of those for whom the appeal of politics was strongest—born, as one contemporary put it, not from a mother but a manifesto. At the time it seemed desperately important, fun too, and immensely satisfying. It did not distract from academic work, for that was another way to acquire levers to move the world. Party discipline came down on members who neglected study: there was, I recall, a priggish slogan—Every Party Member A First! Even sport was turned to account. Rugby or rowing was encouraged as a means of acquiring what was known in the jargon as 'a mass basis'. As an experience it was undoubtedly educational. When, as a journalist, I later began to write about Soviet and East

European politics I had a better idea of how the system worked than if I had read it up second-hand and written examination papers on it. Hindsight can always find useful by-products of youthful enthusiasm.

Many of my contemporaries, of course, had different enthusiasms; they were bored by proselytes and had a much more down-to-earth attitude to student life—though they were cheerfully tolerant of orators and pamphlet-sellers. They played games, gossiped, took themselves off to the Little Rose and searched around for a friendly flat with a spare bed. Cambridge had much to offer them, and the School staff were comfortably relaxed about both politics and sex. They bore agreeably with a din of propaganda that must have privately been disagreeable to many of them—and in matters of morals they were plainly more worried about the susceptibilities of landladies than the behaviour of students. (There was some kind of bush telegraph from The Hostel which always gave adequate notice when, on one of her regular visits as billeting officer to students' accommodation, Vera Anstey was likely to stumble on any irregular establishment.) Carr-Saunders was a remote but likable Director who ran the School in what would now be called 'low-profile' style. Even when he disagreed with you he was reassuring rather than patronizing: puritanical politics and soft sex were not part of his scheme of things, but neither were battles about student rights and discipline. In 1942, when he received a directive from the Ministry of Labour asking for a 'list of names of any students whose conduct and progress have been unsatisfactory and who are in consequence at the disposal of the Ministry' he made the laconic comment: 'Noted.' The School's survival through the strains and shortages of war owed much more than was then apparent to his patient resourcefulness.

It also owed much to its staff, who suddenly found themselves running a residential college—but under wartime conditions—and that new role demanded a great deal. They had to carry a heavy teaching load: Laski, Kahn-Freund and Ginsberg, for example, regularly spent up to twenty hours a week on lectures, seminars and tutorials. They had additional obligations, such as Vera Anstey's superbly smooth handling of the tricky matter of billets, or firewatching, or various bits of Government work done part-time, or sorting out the official instructions about call-up, and paper shortages, and rationing, that rained out of Whitehall. And they were already planning the School after the war. From 1940 onwards, with incongruous optimism, the Professorial Council was discussing new degree structures, research policy, the future of the library, student residences and the constitution of the Union. But the greatest change, I believe, was in relationships. There was a relaxed intimacy with students (more common today, but less usual in the 'thirties) which more than compensated for the difficulty of offering something like a full curriculum with depleted resources. Staff and students felt a sense of mutual accessibility, which knitted them together intellectually as well as socially. One reflection of wartime styles was the feeling (enhanced by the knowledge one might soon be in a military camp or a factory) that academic work really mattered.

No one contributed more to this mood than Harold Laski. In my case, as a specialist in government, his vivid personality coloured all my experience of the School. In Houghton Street he was an assertive, controversial figure, but only one among many other eminent and articulate colleagues. In Cambridge, as one of the few senior members of staff who taught full-time through the war, he stood apart. He was then at the peak of his reputation, both academically and in Labour politics— and that combination of personal teaching and public preaching was peculiarly suited to the mood of wartime. He was, to use one of his own favourite quotations, 'a brooding omnipresence' in the Cambridge scene. His lectures were crammed. Outside his room over a chemist's shop in King's Parade there was always a queue of students (not merely his own tutees) waiting for an interview. He was a familiar sight in the Cambridge streets, a little man walking stiffly like a dark-suited marionette to Mill Lane or Grove Lodge, that small cartoonable face of moustache and round spectacles tucked under a black homburg that always seemed two sizes too big for him. He drove himself hard, for a man who was never in good health. Apart from his teaching in Cambridge, he carried a staggering load of speech-making and committee-work for the Labour Party. Up and down the country he went, to cold halls, in dark and crowded trains, doing as much as any man in the party to keep Labour propaganda alive through the political truce. And somehow he also found time to write—regular articles in the *New Statesman*, for the *Nation* and *New Republic* in America, and half-a-dozen books, political pot-boilers no doubt, but none the less influential at the time.

He was, above all else, a great teacher—especially if one judges a teacher by the power to excite and motivate. I never saw a lecturer who could hold an audience better. His set-pieces were word-perfect; even the jokes had been evacuated to Cambridge. They were nevertheless extraordinary perform-ances, delivered in the high-pitched inflected cadences that made him sound as though he were reciting. The complex syntax rolled on as he stood, almost motionless, the fingers of his right hand dipped into a waistcoat pocket, the left hand grasping his lapel, as if the sentences had been long ago rolled up inside him and were now unwound at the touch of a spring. He gave the same sense of intimacy with the eminent dead as he did with the eminent living. He talked of Hobbes, Locke, Rousseau, Marx and Bentham as if he had lunched with them yesterday, just as he gave the impression in his private con-versation that Churchill, Roosevelt, Attlee, Morrison, Justice Frankfurter and Ed Murrow were all waiting to get him on the telephone when he had a spare moment. Certainly he was vain; undoubtedly many of his stories were apocryphal; in-disputably he was a name-dropper. His friends as well as his critics knew that he was given to flights of fantasy. He talked too much, and he talked at you too much. When you went into his room for a tutorial you would be greeted with that familiar phrase: 'Before you tell me what you've been doing, I want to tell you . . .' which would precede some embroidered anecdote. Yet behind the groomed vanity there was genuine compassion and kindness. He would take endless trouble with his students, sometimes generous with money as well as with practical help, advice or introduction. He was fair-minded, never using his intellectual superiority to crush a halting argument or a shaky case. Enough of his stories were true and all of them were sufficiently interesting to grip one's attention and give a sense of vicarious involvement with the great and the good. Above all, Laski was the epitome of the theory and practice of government and so many students strove to emulate him—to stroll, so to speak, down the corridors of power as well as in the groves of academe.

If he had a serious fault as a teacher it was in this incitement to emulate, though at the time that stimulus seemed a virtue. It made one strive—so much that students unconsciously mimicked his speech and mannerisms—and it made one feel important by association. It was achieved by a combination of flattery and intellectual seduction. One can understand why, despite his unprepossessing appearance and high-flown verbosity, Laski was a star performer at Labour Party meetings.

He was, nevertheless, scrupulously careful not to exploit this power for political purposes within the School. He had a strong sense of academic propriety. Privately, he encouraged Labour Party members who found it hard to wrestle with the Lacöonic coils of the Communist Party; I can only remember one public occasion when he openly intervened in student politics. One Saturday morning, when the campaign for the People's Convention was at its height, he walked into his ten-o'clock lecture in Mill Lane and announced that he proposed to take a contemporary document as a case-study. For the next hour he dissected a twopenny pamphlet by R. Palme Dutt in a brilliant impromptu polemic against communist policy. Otherwise the roles of professor and politician were properly distinguished. Laski may have been ambiguous about the relationship of Marxism and democracy—a dualism which gave interest to his writings in the 'thirties, makes them seem dated now, and was the direct cause of his downfall in the libel case cross-examination by Sir Patrick Hastings—but he never wavered in a belief in civil liberty. He had got into trouble at Harvard at the outset of his academic career for supporting a police strike. He had been under great pressure from Sir William Beveridge, the Director of the School in the 'twenties and early 'thirties, who disliked his staff involving themselves in journalism and politics—especially socialist pamphleteering and public speaking. And as a member of the Labour Party executive Laski had seen Stafford Cripps and Anuerin Bevan expelled for supporting the Popular Front. Within the School he stood squarely for free thought and free speech. The only difficulty in a seminar or a tutorial was finding space between his words to speak oneself.

Harold Laski was the focal point of my LSE. Lawyers, sociologists, historians and economists no doubt formed other personal and academic relationships which were as meaningful to them—with Ginsberg, for instance, or Lance Beales, Bill Pickles or Kahn-Freund. I was caught by the engaging conservative eccentricities of George Schwarz, touched by the winsome kindness of May Wallas, impressed by something profound in R. H. Tawney. But all of us were unavoidably swung to some degree into orbit around Laski. He, more than anyone else, exemplified the School in the war years. He was worn out when they were over.

How to sum up what I and others took away from Laski and his colleagues? Despite wartime conditions they gave us nothing second-rate, no specifications pared down to 'utility' standards. They created an environment in which it was easy to learn, and fun to learn—and these are the conditions in which students flourish. I cannot say whether it was a worse or better experience than Houghton Street; I can only say it was different and profoundly satisfying. Even if examination criteria are notionally constant, one cannot usefully compare student generations. The intake varies, so does mood, motivation, effect. But one rough test may be the subsequent emergence from that wartime cohort of students of a significant group of academics. Apart from Tibor Barna and Heinz Arndt—both economists of distinction whom I should perhaps exclude because they had started as research students just before the war—I can think off-hand of almost a dozen who went on to professorships: O. R. Macgregor, Claus Moser and Hal Myint in London, Chris Freeman and Bernard Shaffer at Sussex, Ralph Miliband at Leeds, Stanley Benn at Canberra, others who returned to posts in Europe and the Third World. Ken Berrill went on to a Cambridge Fellowship and the chairmanship of the University Grants Committee before becoming the head of the Government's Think Tank; Eprime Eshag made his mark at the United Nations before returning to Oxford for a Wadham Fellowship. And Margaret Petrie, May Ravden, Peter Richards and Pearl Veerhault are only a few of those I still meet as colleagues or in the journals and publishers' lists.

Since academics naturally beget academics, a better measure may be success in other fields, where future careers are anyway less easy to predict. An interval of war service also made it harder to guess thirty-five years ago where chance and ability would take the majority. The obvious bet that a number of such a politically-minded generation would go directly into politics proved wrong. (Surprisingly few LSE graduates seem to become practising politicians. When I recently looked through the list of all School graduates in this century I was astonished how few have gone into Parliament.) Jack Mendelson was clearly headed for the House of Commons. He was not only the outstanding speaker of his day, but the most avid reader of newspapers I have ever known. When he joined the army it took several hands to carry the piles of foreign newspapers to a Cambridge fishmonger: for months the frozen cod came wrapped in pre-war copies of *Le Temps*, the *Corriere della Sera* and the *New York Herald Tribune*. Lyndell Evans and

Bee Katz were similarly cut-out for careers as Labour coun-
cillors, though who could have anticipated the latter's metamorphosis as Lady Serota, the Ombudsman for Local
Government?

Perhaps I should have been sure that Ken Sykora, already
a good enough guitarist to play with Geraldo's band at the
weekends in his first year, would find a career in the jazz
world; that Tony Simmons, always more anxious to discuss
an unfinished play than read for his law examinations, would
end up as a film director—and that Steve Wheatcroft, with
equal skills as a pilot and an economist, would rise to the top
of British Airways. Perhaps there was a link between Hugh
Burnett's brilliance as cartoonist for the wall-newspaper *Beaver*
and as director of 'Face to Face'. But what about Vladimir
Raitz and Gordon Brunton: was a common passion for poker
the real predictor of Raitz's ability to build Horizon Holidays
almost single-handed or of Brunton's emergence as a key man
in the Thomson organization? What student of form would
have picked Elwyn Jones as the creator of Barlow and 'Z-Cars',
David Davis as a World Bank expert on tourism, Leslie Finer—
in Athens as the correspondent of the *Observer* and the BBC—
as the man the Colonels hated, or Arnold Weinstock as
Britain's most successful industrialist?

In retrospect one looks for clues. Claus Moser's musical
talent points as directly to the chairmanship of Covent Garden
as his academic abilities led to the Robbins Committee and the
directorship of the Central Statistical Office. But in this game
of who-was-to-become-who my favourite entry is Joe Yagchi,
known for his playboy charm, his commitment to Newmarket,
and a knowledge of economics so narrow that his cheerful one-
word explanation of every phenomenon in the economy was
'Inflation'. He was, therefore, better prepared for the post-
war world than some of us, and appropriately became one of
Kuwait's commercial representatives.

One day the portly Russian sniper Ludmilla Pavlichenko
descended on Grove Lodge on a propaganda tour. It was one

of those 'goodwill' visits where one exchanged platitudes through an interpreter, though it then seemed a portentous moment. The Union had decided to present her with a volume of Shakespeare as a souvenir. Something had to be inscribed in it and Joy Reed, then president of the Union, leafed quickly through for an appropriate quotation. She came up with the Agincourt speech—'we few, we happy few, we band of brothers . . .'—and the phrase was duly written on the flyleaf. It fitted the mood of the day. It fitted the mood of the evacuees at Clare-Market-on-the-Cam much better and more enduringly.

J. W. N. Watkins

John Watkins was born in 1924 and from 1946–49 was a student at the London School of Economics. From 1938–41 he was at the Royal Naval College, Dartmouth and from 1941–46 he served as midshipman, sub-lieutenant, and lieutenant in several ships of the Royal Navy. In 1944 he was awarded the D.S.C. for torpedoing a German destroyer in the English Channel. During 1949–50 he was Henry Ford Fellow at Yale University. He has taught at the London School of Economics since 1950 and is now Professor of Philosophy there. He is the author of Hobbes's System of Ideas *(1965),* Entscheidung und Freiheit *(1977), and many papers in philosophical journals. From 1972–75 he was President of the British Society for the Philosophy of Science.*

I was the navigator of a destroyer, in Sydney, preparing to sail with an invasion fleet to Japan, when I heard of the Bomb on Hiroshima. I was a regular naval officer, ex-Dartmouth, and since going to sea in 1941 I had never envisaged any other life. (At Dartmouth I had had daydreams of being a big figure in the House of Commons or, sometimes, of being a famous writer.) But my naval life had been dominated by the idea of action against the enemy. And now the enemy was, presumably, finished. A naval career was now pointless—unless another war was in the offing. But I found it intolerable that I should have to nurse the idea of another war in order to rekindle my sense of purpose. The conviction became overwhelming: I must get out.

But what would I do?

Our engineering officer, Laurie Vandome, was a graduate of London University and intended to return to university after the war. He convinced me that I too must go to university. But to study what? Economics perhaps? (We spent the winter of 1945–6 in Shanghai, where a runaway inflation developed and I became puzzled about *money*: how does it work and why does it sometimes get out of control?) Or politics? (I had considered myself a socialist and would have voted Labour in the 1945 election if it had not come a few days before my twenty-first birthday. But Vandome lent me Hayek's *Road to*

Serfdom, which transformed my outlook almost overnight. I was now filled with foreboding about the dangers of socialism.)

I forget when I first began to consider LSE.(Perhaps Hayek's being there suggested it to me.) But I remember what clinched it. This was a scene in Evelyn Waugh's *Put Out More Flags*. War had just been declared, and Poppet Green, Ambrose Silk and others are discussing the great controversial issue of the time: the departure of the poets Parsnip and Pimpernell to America. The passage on which I seized was this:

> Thus the aesthetic wrangle might have run its familiar course, but there was in the studio that morning a cross, red-headed girl in spectacles from the London School of Economics . . .
>
> 'What I don't see,' she said . . . 'is how these two can claim to be *Contemporary* if they run away from the biggest event in contemporary history . . . It's just sheer escapism,' she said.
>
> The word startled the studio, like the cry of 'Cheat' in a card-room.

I instantly formed a picture of LSE: it was a place where girls, and especially red-headed girls, impatiently cut through obfuscating highbrow talk to get at the real issue. (I will mention two red-headed girls I met at LSE later.) I would go there.

This was easier said than done. The Admiralty turned down my resignation. My parents were strongly opposed. And it was by no means certain that LSE would take me. I had to fight. Eventually the Admiralty relented: I could leave if I were accepted by LSE. I was accepted. My father generously gave me an allowance of £200 a year. In October 1946 I was a student registered for the B.Sc.(Econ), with a bed-sitting room in a pleasant flat facing Battersea Park.

I wanted to write. (I had been writing some things during my last year in the Navy, including a couple of short stories;

but I decided that fiction was too exhausting for me.) And I wanted to go into politics. My plan was simple: I would seize every opportunity to speak in public; my name would in due course become known in the right quarters; and I would end up in the House of Commons. In the meanwhile I read Monypenny and Buckle's *Life of Disraeli* and joined the LSE Conservative Society (thereby swelling its membership by about ten per cent).

My first opportunity to speak in public was at the opening meeting, in October 1946, of the Students' Union. A striking-looking girl, Kari Polanyi, moved a motion in support of a strike at the Savoy Hotel. (She was a communist, and a very gifted niece of Michael Polanyi.) She spoke movingly and effectively. I spoke against, and was listened to with incredulity. Her motion was carried by 51 to 3.

Things went better at a Student Union debate on Socialism, a few weeks later, where I secured the role of principal opposition speaker. We lost, of course, but only by 43 to 65.

In November there was a by-election in North Paddington and my offer to do open-air speaking for the Conservative candidate was accepted. It was a chilling experience. Indeed, I was actually frightened by the bitter hostility of some of the local people. And I failed a test. One cold, foggy evening we were hanging around our street-corner stand, with no one in sight, when we received a message that Mr Turner, the candidate, would be coming to the stand at 7 pm and wanted us to build up a crowd for him. I was asked to start the process, but I found myself quite incapable of making a speech to an empty street. Someone else did it. A woman stopped, looked at the speaker, looked round for the people he was addressing, and shook her head in disbelief. But she stayed. A couple joined her. Someone heckled; and there were about forty people there when the candidate arrived.

I made some attempts to make myself known to Conservative politicians but they invariably misfired. I secured a meeting with Anthony Nutting (then President of the Young Con-

servatives). We spoke at cross-purposes, he about winning the
next election on food-rationing and 'Socialist misrule', I about
a return to Burkean principles. I stalked out sulkily.

The next Conservative politician I met was Bob Boothby.
He and a Socialist MP called Millington were to be the
principal speakers at another Students' Union debate on
Socialism, in February 1947, and I was to second him. He
arrived exuding bonhomie. My hand was a bit limp after the
introductions: he pumped it vigorously three times over
because I got introduced to him three times. In the debate it
turned out that there was a genial accord between himself and
Millington, who was a Left-wing rebel: both were against the
Government's pretend-planning and wanted some real planning in its place. In my speech I took a Hayekian line against
State ownership and planning as such, and was cheerily
heckled by Boothby. He smoked almost incessantly through
the debate. The power shortage, during that exceptionally cold
winter, had led to a cigarette famine, and I had been driven to
scouring Mayfair tobacconists, lit now by candles, for, say, an
expensive packet of State Express 555 or, once, a terribly
expensive box of 100 Perfectos. Boothby's cigarette-case was
soon empty and I watched gloomily as my own hard-won
packet was steadily depleted. I had hoped that we would
have some conversation afterwards over supper, but Boothby
and Millington had to hurry off to, respectively, Claridges
and the Dorchester. I went disconsolately to the library to read
economics.

In the Easter vacation I went with a London delegation to
a University Conservative Conference at Hoddesdon. The big
speakers were Harold Macmillan and Anthony Eden. Eden
looked askance when I told him that I was from LSE; and it
began to dawn on me that LSE was not the best springboard
for a career in Conservative politics: Oxford or Cambridge
would have been much better. A young man from Oxford, the
Hon Edward Boyle, especially impressed me. His speech was
relaxed, shrewd and humorous. At one point he forgot what

he was saying. That would have thrown me into a panic. But he was quite unperturbed, explaining disarmingly that he had lost the thread. There was a debate on Imperial Preference, which was an article of faith for most of those present. But I was a Free Trader, and I decided to have a go. I had had little time to prepare anything, so I was relieved when my opening remarks caused pandemonium. I concluded by apologizing for interrupting so many members of the audience, which brought clapping and laughter.

At about this time I made one more effort to fulfil my plan. I persuaded the London University Conservatives that we ought to make a splash with a big meeting. This was accepted and it was decided that the main speaker should be Harold Macmillan. As the second speaker I suggested Aubrey Jones (whom I regarded as something of a prototype: an intellectual Conservative who had studied politics under Laski, as I intended to do). This was agreed. I was chosen as the third speaker. A large hall was booked.

In my daydreams the meeting went something like this. Aubrey Jones speaks first, a solid, thoughtful speech which wins considerable applause. Macmillan speaks next. His speech is wittier and more polished, and wins rather more applause. Then I speak. At first the audience is suspicious of this unknown stripling from (of all unsuitable places) LSE. But my first joke brings a ripple of laughter . . . I end on a passionate note and sit down amid tumultuous applause. Too big a man to feel envy, Macmillan leans across and says: 'We need people like you in the House.'

As the day drew nearer this dream gave way to panic. Our membership was small and I feared that there would be only a sprinkling of people in the hall. I pressed invitations on everyone I could think of. And what on earth was I to speak about? If only I had been given a motion to speak to, instead of carte blanche.

In the event the occasion fulfilled neither my worst fears nor my best hopes. The hall was nearly full and I made a tolerable speech. But Macmillan, who spoke first and very well, slipped away as soon as he decently could. My plan was no nearer fulfilment.

Actually, by the time this meeting took place (October 28, 1947) my plan was already beginning to fade: I was growing disenchanted with the idea of a life in politics. There were various reasons. It had partially dawned on me that a lot of drudgery in committee rooms and on doorsteps would be necessary if I were to get anywhere. Another reason was that, although I had met quite a few people during my year of pushful political activity, I had not formed friendships with any of them. The people I came to like and respect at LSE were all more or less scornful of party politics, or at least of Conservative Party politics. Finally, with my Intermediate examinations out of the way and free to concentrate on what interested me, I was becoming fascinated by the new worlds of ideas that were opening up. One day, as I walked past what was then the Battersea Polytechnic, I wondered whether I might perhaps get a job there. The idea of an academic life was supplanting the idea of a political one.

I now looked back on that first year with a kind of shudder. My speechifying now seemed empty and juvenile. (Actually, I had learnt something of the art of public speaking. For instance, I learnt not to over-prepare. I once rehearsed a speech until I was word perfect. When I gave it I felt like an automaton and my mouth became dry.) I had been slow to make friends and I was often lonely and unhappy. But I never questioned my decision to leave the Navy. I did not yet feel at home in this strange new world but I felt completely estranged from the old one.

During my last days in the Navy I had met a Wren, Geraldine Hughesden, who was also going to LSE. She now had a flat near the British Museum which she shared with Valerie Hughes (one of the two red-headed girls I mentioned earlier). I was fond of Geraldine and my social life during my first months at LSE largely consisted of cups of coffee at their flat.

They must have found me a trying visitor: I was so starved of social intercourse that I talked and talked when I was there. My idea of an outing for Geraldine was to take her to a lecture by Bertrand Russell on 'Philosophy and Politics'. I was bowled over by the man himself and by what he said. (I found myself very critical of the lecture, ten years later, when I reread it in connection with something I was writing.) The next time I heard Russell speak was at LSE shortly after he had had to swim ashore when his flying-boat sank in an icy Norwegian fjord. We gave him an ovation. (I heard afterwards that when this feat was reported to G. E. Moore he replied: '*I* could have done that.')

I cannot recall that period without thinking of the tram I took from Battersea to Holborn. It was quick; but it rattled and clattered; and it *smelt*, a fact which I imputed, perhaps unfairly, to the elderly women, dressed in black, who eyed me morosely when I sat down and buried my head in Benham's *Economics* or Crowther's *Outline of Money*. During the big freeze in early 1947 the points jammed at Nine Elms and I would have to walk the last bit through the snow in leaky shoes.

The couple from whom I rented my room, Frank and Gwen White, treated me almost as a member of the family. He was a civil servant and she was a teacher. Although they were Labour supporters they took an encouraging interest in what I did. As soon as I had finished a piece I would take it to them for appraisal, hot from my battered typewriter (which I had bought in Sydney along with a book on How to Write).

Another person who helped me to get outside myself was Alan Stuart, with whom I struck up a friendship in my second term. With him also I talked and talked, but he talked back. I learnt a lot from him. His interests were wider than mine, and he was more cultured. He was another person who would always read my latest piece. He was sharply critical and often advised me, with reason, to scrap it.

In my second year at LSE I felt more at home and became more sociable. I belonged, now, to the Government Department and, with John Grist, was put onto a departmental committee whose meetings were friendly. I was in a political thought class, run by Bill Pickles, where the discussion was unusually good. And some of us, including Kenneth Topley and Geoffrey Engholm, formed a discussion group of our own. Later, this was joined by Alan Milne. He had been blinded towards the end of the war and I got to know him by being one of those who took it in turns to read to him.

And the situation in the Students' Union changed radically in my second year. When I first came to LSE there had been one Popular Front organization, called Soc Soc, to cater for all shades of Leftist opinion, but managed by people on the far Left; and Soc Soc, in turn, dominated the Union. (At the last election for President of the Students' Union there had been three seemingly independent candidates, but I discovered that they were all communists.) For instance, Zilliacus gave a speech at the Union, deploring Bevin's foreign policy and urging collaboration with the Soviet bloc, which aroused a fervour of approval. But there was one dissentient: a student who had lived for a year in an Iron Curtain country said he was behind Bevin, having observed for himself the effects of communist terror. I overheard a girl in front of me say to her neighbour: 'What's the Chairman doing? Why doesn't he stop him?'

Labour moderates became more and more restive. Many of them were ex-servicemen (at least one was an ex-colonel) and they did not like being manipulated. They broke away from Soc Soc and formed Lab Soc, leaving behind a rump of only thirty or so communists and fellow-travellers.

Their anti-communist attitude was hardened by what happened in Czechoslovakia in February 1948. Jan Masaryk's suicide (as we took it to be: I am now persuaded that he was thrown out of that Prague window) seemed to symbolize the cruel tragedy. The Left-wing line that the Iron Curtain was a product of Churchill's over-heated imagination and that the People's Democracies, unlike capitalist 'democracies', were genuinely democratic, suffered a dramatic refutation. We held an emergency Union debate. I could tell that the Left were worried because they put up some West African students (whose colour would ensure them a respectful hearing) to read out prepared speeches. I was exasperated by some liberals who said that it would be premature to condemn what had happened since we did not know all the facts yet. I pointed out that their over-scrupulousness would paralyse resistance to communism since we never know all the facts. I now spoke, not in my previous jokey, point-scoring way, but seriously and urgently. And for the first time in the Union I had the warming experience of meeting widespread support and approval. The Left suffered a major defeat.

I now got onto an easy footing with some of the leading Lab Soc people, including Sidney Irvine, Pat Duffy and John Stonehouse (all to become Labour MPs). At one concerning the threat of further communist take-overs in Europe, we could afford to bicker good-humouredly over domestic issues. Stonehouse had recently launched *The Student Observer* and he asked me to write for it a case against Labour, which I did.

At about this time there was a vacancy on the Union Council. A communist had been nominated and so had an angry and rhetorical Labour man to whom I was allergic. I was asked to stand. My vanity was tickled. A year ago it would have been inconceivable that I, a notorious Conservative, should be elected. But now I decided to risk it. I was amazed when I got an absolute majority. The existing members of the Council were all communists. They were conscientious and hard-working and we got along well enough. After one drawn-out meeting in the evening we went to the White Horse and had a good deal of beer. A fair, buxom girl with a jolly laugh allowed me to put my arm round her waist. At closing time I had a decision to make: if I were to keep my arm there I would have to dance along the pavement, singing the Red Flag. I did this.

I did not stand at the next election. Once was enough;

and I was, by now, too interested in the new ideas I was trying
to absorb to have much time for Union politics. At this election
the newly formed Lab Soc was determined to prove its strength
by seeing to it that, as far as possible, only candidates approved
by it were elected. One person who felt that its caucus methods
had gone too far was Bernard Levin, and he decided to expose
them. His first step was to get a non-existent 'student' enrolled
as a paid-up member of Lab Soc; then he nominated this
unperson for election to the Union Council. Levin was not a
member of Lab Soc; but his 'candidate' was and that was
enough to secure his inclusion on the list of approved candidates
circulated to Lab Soc members. Nominators of candidates
were required by Union rules to place on the notice-board a
short statement about the candidate, together with a photograph, and to present him in person at the Union meeting
prior to the election. Successful candidates also presented
themselves at the meeting after the election. Levin's 'candidate'
had, it seemed, been a hard-working member of the table-
tennis club. His photograph was blurred. He was unfortunately
unable to be present at the Union meeting, so Levin told us,
because he had flu; but he was a man in whom we could have
every confidence. He was duly elected. (Actually, he only just
scraped in, with the one successful communist just ahead of
him.) At the next meeting this straw man was wheeled onto
the platform by Levin and they received an ovation.

If the Left were down they were by no means out. There
was a period when they had The Three Tuns (our student
common room, now replaced by a tower block) festooned
with grim photographs, allegedly of fascist atrocities in Greece
and elsewhere. One showed a prisoner about to be beheaded:
the man with the axe was grinning. Whether he was the
fascist and his victim the communist or the other way round,
it was a shocking picture, and I ate my sandwiches in a sub-
dued mood.

In my second year I began to rediscover what a marvellous
thing it can be to *read*. From my bedsitter in Battersea I could

glimpse worlds of which I had had no conception. For a time I was attracted by mediaeval thought: it seemed so well organized and clear-cut. (No doubt the picture I formed was very simplistic.) Then I began to look, however amateurishly, into Greek thought. By comparison, the mediaeval scene appeared grey and bureaucratic. Greek thinkers were so much more daring and original.

I also went through an intensive ethical phase. I was without religion and still felt strangely rootless. The thought of Nazi concentration camps and gas-chambers preyed on me. Surely what happened there was not merely bad relative to our liberal standards, but intrinsically and objectively bad. It seemed terribly important to me that values exist 'out there', independently of our personal tastes. I devoured G. E. Moore's *Principia Ethica*, with its seeming demonstration of the autonomy of goodness, and was shocked to learn from 'Jonk' Jonckheere (who often came over from UCL, where he was studying under Ayer) that there was a school of logical positivists who interpreted moral expressions in a 'boo-hurray' way.

I sometimes suffered *Doubts*. Coming out of Waterloo I was nearly knocked down by a lorry as I wrestled with the following dilemma. If the moral order is objective and absolute, it is unchanging and therefore existed before there were people to obey it; but moral imperatives addressed to a mindless universe were all too reminiscent of that speech to an empty street-corner in North Paddington. But if the moral order evolved together with the human race, it is not absolute. In Aldwych I hit upon a solution which brought me immense relief: moral laws are absolute and timeless but they are conditional rather than categorical. They were not forever shouting Do's and Don't's at a mindless universe. They were saying, 'Where there are people this should be done and that should not be done.'

Around November 1947 a friend, Alan Gander, asked me if I was going to Dr Popper's lectures. I wasn't. 'It's worth going,' he said, 'to hear the great man thinking aloud.' The first time I

went he was explaining Poincaré's conventionalist interpretation of Newton's mechanics. It was a glimpse of another new
world of ideas. I was riveted. I had experienced some memorable lecturing at LSE. Lionel Robbins always dominated us
when he gave his 'Principles' course in the Old Theatre. And I
loved the precision and dry humour of James Meade's lectures
on international trade. (I will say something about Laski's
lecturing in a moment.) But Popper's lecturing seemed to me
to be in a category of its own. He spoke, uncluttered by notes
or other paraphernalia, with a peculiar intensity and urgency,
his words falling so exactly into place that one seemed to be
hearing the ideas themselves. As he developed an idea he often
made humorous discoveries which tickled him as much as us.
On one occasion he was discussing whether 'All men are mortal'
is falsifiable. Would it be falsified if a man lands, all smiles,
after having had an atom-bomb exploded under him? (Pause;
new idea; sudden smile.) 'We ask him how he did it and he
says, "Oh, it's easy, I'm immortal." '

However, I was studying politics, not philosophy, and Laski
still dominated my academic horizon, though in an ambiguous
way. I regarded him with a mixture of scepticism and fascination.

When I joined the Government Department Alan Stuart
told me that I ought to make a thorough study of my professor's
works. (This advice proved important for me later.) But Laski
was a prolific writer, and in the end I confined myself to an
examination of his thinking since 1931. I sent the result,
entitled 'Laski on Conscience and Counter-Revolution', to him
and nervously awaited his response. He returned it with the
comment that he was not sure that I had entirely understood
him.

Reading Popper and Hayek had persuaded me that doctrinal
conflicts in politics are usually the result of underlying disagreements at a philosophical level. So the first thing for a
political thinker to do was to get his philosophy right. I even
supposed that once he had done this a sound political theory

J. W. N. WATKINS

77

would develop naturally out of his philosophy. (I did not notice that I was committing Moore's 'naturalistic fallacy'.) Well then, what was I waiting for? It was only a matter of finding the philosophical truths from which an enlightened conservatism would follow. My title would be 'Towards a Philosophy of Conservatism'. The writing went quite briskly at first as I laid down absolutist premises about truth and values; but the pace got slower and slower as I tried to proceed from these to the desired political conclusions. The thing became a nightmare. Eventually I brought it to some sort of conclusion and sent it to Laski. He returned it without comment. I don't blame him. It was heavy and pretentious (its paragraphs were numbered in the manner of Wittgenstein's *Tractatus*, no doubt in a subconscious attempt to hide the paucity of logical connections). But it seems that he took some notice of it. In a talk on socialism to new students at the beginning of the next term he said that many serious thinkers had contributed to socialism, but only three to conservatism: 'Edmund Burke, Lord Hugh Cecil, and John Watkins, a student of this School'!

My estimate of Laski fluctuated considerably during my three years as a student. His first year lectures on the British Constitution were a delight: racy, sardonic, anecdotal. But I was disenchanted, in my second year, by his specialist lectures on political thought. He would stand, practically motionless, holding one small sheet by way of notes, speaking with an expressionless face. (I was reminded of Monypenny and Buckle's description of Disraeli's parliamentary style.) There were no false starts, hesitations, or other signs that he was thinking it through as he spoke. It was as if he were reading from a teleprompter. Some of his sentences were so labyrinthine (with, say, an allegedly verbatim quotation, plus the page-reference, within a parenthetical aside to a subordinate clause) that it was a marvel to us that he brought them, as he invariably did, to a grammatically successful conclusion. The effect on me was the opposite of Popper's effect: the words smothered

the ideas. On one occasion he embarked on the wrong lecture.
After a few minutes someone pointed this out. He paused, put
away his notes, took out new ones, and the smooth flow
immediately recommenced, this time on the scheduled subject.
I was amazed. My view of him changed again in my third
year, when I began to have some personal contact with him.

During much of my third year I was in a state of near-
manic excitement and activity. I had returned from the summer
vacation with a draft entitled 'Hobbes's Method'. I had the
feeling that I was on to something serious, discovering politically interesting implications in philosophical ideas instead of
trying to force desired conclusions out of them. I went on
working at this paper through the year. I pressed it, at one
stage or another, on a lot of people. (In those days I had no
compunction about importuning people with my stuff.) I also
started a political science club, which involved a good deal of
work, but was very rewarding. I got A. J. P. Taylor, Michael
Oakeshott, Michael Polanyi, and Denis Brogan to speak at it.
Polanyi's paper, 'Scientific Convictions', made a deep impression on me. (It became Chapter Two of his *The Logic of
Liberty*.) For Oakeshott's paper, 'Rational Conduct', I felt an
uneasy admiration. (It became Chapter Four of his *Rationalism
in Politics*. It takes off from a Victorian writer's claim that
bloomers are the rational dress for women cyclists.) I persuaded
Popper to come to this meeting. In the discussion he was
making a criticism when Oakeshott interrupted with 'But what
do you mean by——?', picking on a word Popper had used.
When Popper tried to explain, Oakeshott again interrupted
with 'But what do you mean by——?', now picking on a word
Popper had used in explanation of the first word. This went
on for some time and the audience got restive. Finally Popper
ended the regress by answering, 'Oh, I mean by it what you
mean by it.'

Laski in his seminar was very different from Laski in the
lecture-room: eager, volatile, now lighting up with enthusiasm,
now growling morosely, sometimes unfair, and often pungent.

('Except on Bruno's', he interjected, when someone stated that Giordano Bruno's ideas had had little influence on men's lives.) He ran the seminar in a makeshift way, often picking on someone to state a view there and then, or at the next meeting. He often picked on me, and we had some fierce battles: he had an intense dislike for the ideas of most of my then intellectual heroes, except for Collingwood, for whom he had a high regard. Although he deplored many of my ideas, he treated me with great generosity and warmth, calling me a 'find' and encouraging me to take up an academic career; he advised me, as a first step, to try for a scholarship at a major American university, which I did.

I first attended Popper's seminar on November 4, 1948, after hearing that a New Zealand student of his, Helen Hervey, was giving a paper on Hobbes. John Passmore was also there. I found that in this seminar what mattered was not so much the papers as the remarkable, and often devastating interventions they provoked from Popper. (However, Shirley Letwin gave a very good paper on the Webbs which was not interrupted once: a unique achievement.) In January there was a hole in the programme and I was able to give part of my Hobbes paper. It was hotly criticized. I realized it would need a lot of redoing. (I was to go on redoing it for fifteen years.) After this seminar I went to Popper, rather diffidently, to discuss my American applications. I found him very approachable. He wrote out a testimonial for me, then decided that it was not quite right, and did another which again did not satisfy him. So he did a third version, telling me in the meanwhile that he had written *The Open Society* some thirty times. In those days he had an evening lecture, and after this meeting I sometimes had supper with him in the Barley Sugar room. I had an obsessive desire to discuss ethics. He would patiently forbear with this for a while, sharply criticizing, say, Moore's aestheticism, and then switch the conversation to Attlee, or foreign policy, or (most often) Russia. He had the knack of English understatement: e.g. 'Not my cup of tea' (after my summary description of a continental thinker then in vogue) or, 'The English tradition is not so bad.'

I had submitted 'Laski on Conscience and Counter-Revolution' to *The Nineteenth Century and After* (as what is now *The Twentieth Century* was then obliged to call itself) for an undergraduate essay prize, and it won. It appeared in March 1949, shortly before I was interviewed for a Henry Ford scholarship. (There were four of these, two for Harvard and two for Yale; they were of considerable value, and they usually went to Oxbridge candidates.) One of the interviewers had read this essay; it probably tipped the balance: I was their fourth choice, assigned to Yale.

Its tone was abrasive and Laski was cooler to me after it appeared, but only briefly. (In a broadcast tribute later, Carr-Saunders gave as an instance of Laski's liberalism his continued support for a student who had harshly criticized him in print.) Not long after this he was urging me to take care of my health. (I smoked too much and was pale.) He once left the seminar for an injection, remarking that the drug had saved his life. How dependent I felt on this, for me improbable, father-figure was brought home to me a year later, at Yale, when I came across his photograph on the obituary page of *The Times*: I felt as though I had been hit. (I was reading Freud's *Interpretation of Dreams* at the time. When I went to bed I resolved not to indulge in any wish-fulfilment dream about him; and I did not. I repeated this the next night, with the same result. The third night I took no precaution and dreamt that Laski was offering me a stunning job. When I woke up I was disgusted with myself.)

I was not successful with girls. Geraldine suddenly married another man. I became very close to her ex-flat mate Valerie, but there was no sexual attraction in it. She had a kindly, mocking humour; she was everyone's confidante and, I am sure, knew much more about the weaknesses and foibles of people in her wide circle than anyone else; but this knowledge only enhanced, for her, the interest and value of the people in

question. (An amiable weakness of hers was that she was rather
ashamed of the fact that she had been a very athletic school-
girl.) For me she was a centre of sanity, a friendly, unpaid
psychotherapist to whom I very often had recourse, especially
when I was feeling low. (Alas, that sanity of hers began to
break up about ten years later, and she committed suicide.)

Another girl of whom I became very fond was Joanna
Cartledge, who was a year ahead of me on the Government
course. She played the cello. In those days of utility clothing
she dressed with elegant audacity. Outwardly, she appeared
cool, fastidious, detached, looking as if she had wandered from
some more exotic place into these drab surroundings, and then
elected to stay for a while because of their human interest. In
the summer we sometimes ambled through Mayfair streets. I
liked looking at the outsides of places I had been inside during
short leaves in wartime, when I had briefly had money to
burn. Whatever we talked about, the conversation tended to
turn eventually to Roman Catholicism, to which she was
inclining. I strenuously opposed this, but to no avail. The fact
was that there was another man, and he was a Roman Catholic.

Near the end of 1948 Valerie had a new flat-mate, an LSE
graduate who was now a research student. Her appearance
startled me: she had beautiful red hair. Her name was Micky
Roe. I became an even more frequent visitor at 32 Museum
Chambers. (We married, later.)

Final examinations began on June 13, the three compulsory
economics papers coming first. I coped well enough with the
'Principles' and 'Applied' papers, but the 'History' paper
posed a problem. I had planned to scrape through this on the
knowledge acquired for the Intermediate paper two years
earlier. But the questions were entirely different: there was
not one for which I had even the beginnings of an answer.
Should I walk out? I decided to try gamesmanship. (I was
rather shocked to discover, later, that I got an upper second
on this paper.) I tore into the specialist papers with maniacal
energy. By Friday evening I was done for; but there was still

one paper to come, on Monday afternoon. I dragged myself
to the room. The questions I wanted were there, but I could
hardly goad myself to write out my prepared answers.

The results were posted a month later. I had a First. With
this on top of my essay prize and Henry Ford scholarship, I
ought to have been on top of the world. But I wasn't. Breaking
free of the Navy and coming to LSE had been an arduous
business, and I had half-hated the place at first. And now, just
as I was feeling at home in it, I had to make another break. I
did not know that I would be back a year later, to stay.

Robert McKenzie

Robert McKenzie is Professor of Sociology with special reference to Politics at LSE, where he was a postgraduate student from 1947–49, and member of staff from 1949. He has also taught at the University of British Columbia where he obtained his first degree, and as a visiting lecturer at Harvard and Yale. He is the author of British Political Parties: The Distribution of Power within the Conservative and Labour Parties, *and, with Allan Silver, of* Angels in Marble: Working-Class Conservatism in England. *He also broadcasts on contemporary politics.*

It would be impossible to disentangle my recollections of my days as a postgraduate student at LSE which began in 1947 from my memories of life in London during and just after the Second War. I doubt if there could have been a more exciting place and time in which to return to university life. I had had the offer of a place at Peterhouse, Cambridge; and I had to make up my mind whether to go there or to LSE. I was twenty-nine; I had had an enormously varied and interesting ten years (four of them in the Canadian army) since I got my first degree at the University of British Columbia in Vancouver; I simply could not see myself settling into the strongly undergraduate-oriented life at Cambridge. England's two ancient universities (dealt with earlier in this series),* tend to treat higher education as a cottage industry, turning out hand-made minds. Whatever the advantages of this system for 18-year-olds just out of school—and I think they can be easily exaggerated—it was clearly, I decided, not for me.

*I found it in no way surprising that the School has been accorded third place in this series. I first understood the pecking order of British universities when I read the results of a contest in the *New Statesman*, twenty-odd years ago. Bertrand Russell, said the rubric, once declined the following irregular verb: '*I* am firm; *you* are stubborn; *he* is a pig-headed fool.' Contestants were invited to submit entries based on this model. One of the winning entries read: '*I* am Oxford; *you* are Cambridge; *he* is the London School of Economics.'

I was already under the spell of London where I had lived intermittently during the years 1944–46 while attached to Canadian Military Headquarters; I was certain that I wanted to do postgraduate research on some aspect of the British party system, and the ideal base of operations was clearly LSE. Its location is unrivalled: half an hour's walk from Parliament, Whitehall and the party headquarters in Smith Square, with Fleet Street and the City a few minutes away in the other direction. The School has what is probably the best social science library in Europe and the British Museum is close at hand. When one adds to all this the cultural resources of London, then in the midst of a very remarkable renaissance especially in the performing arts, it will not be difficult to understand how I arrived at my decision.

I can recall almost to the day when I had first fallen under the spell of LSE. It was an evening in Vancouver in the spring of 1939 when I was a teaching assistant at the University of British Columbia. I had been attending the lectures of a visiting professor, Ivor Jennings of LSE, the leading authority on the British constitution. Jennings took the chair at a public lecture addressed by his most famous colleague, Professor Harold Laski, then on a North American lecture tour. Subsequently I was privileged to be present, wide-eyed, when the two men discussed the prospects for peace and war in Europe, the condition of British politics, and in passing, the domestic news of LSE.

I had been aware of the attractions of the School through talking with Dr Sylvia Thrupp, who had studied with Eileen Power at LSE, and who taught me medieval history. I also felt myself vicariously involved in the British political scene as a result of avid reading of the *New Statesman*, the *Manchester Guardian*, the *Political Quarterly* and even *Tribune* (whose earliest copies of 1937 had been given to me by an immigrant English friend). I agreed with their bitter criticisms of the policy of appeasement; and in addition I had undoubtedly been influenced by the neo-isolationism of Left-wing Canadian intellectuals like Frank Scott of McGill and Frank Underhill of the University of Toronto. On recently re-reading my diaries for 1938–39, I find that I held the view that Britain under Chamberlain was on a suicidal course; that after Munich, Canada as an independent nation ought to clarify its right to neutrality in the event that appeasement led to war, and should coordinate her policies closely with the Roosevelt Government in Washington. But Laski in his lecture forced us to re-consider the world crisis from the European viewpoint; he made us think about issues such as the fate of the Jews, of the trade unionists and of the political Left under Hitler, all of which were too easily evaded by the North American Left of that time. And as always he stated his case with such style and panache that the impact of his lectures, particularly on student audiences, was enormous.

Contrary to what has sometimes been claimed, it was possible to admire Laski without necessarily succumbing to all his own beliefs; certainly then, and subsequently when I studied under him, I was in basic disagreement with him on a wide range of issues and in my experience he relished rather than resented it when his students disagreed with him. For the past twenty years I have been a 'floating voter' (or as I would prefer to put it a 'tactical voter') and have found myself voting at one election or another for each of the three major parties; but when I first met Laski I was a committed social democrat, rather in the mould of my near contemporaries, whom of course I had never met, Roy Jenkins and Anthony Crosland. I had been thoroughly innoculated against the wide-spread tendency in those years to idealize Soviet communism, in part through the odd good fortune of having an elderly, largely self-educated Polish neighbour in Vancouver who showered me with Trotskyite literature. Whatever its shortcomings it did at least anticipate by twenty years the exposé of the terror under Stalin which Kruschev was to provide at the Twentieth Congress of the Communist Party of the Soviet Union. In Canadian politics my sympathies lay with the Cooperative

Commonwealth Federation (CCE), a social democratic party founded in 1934, which had fraternal links with the British Labour Party and which shared its opposition to both the United Front and later the Popular Front.

On such issues as the nature of Soviet society and the Popular Front I thought Laski was plainly wrong but this did not alter my eagerness to study under him. Although I had not thought seriously until then of the possibility of studying at LSE, I found myself that spring evening in 1939 telling Laski that it was the one overriding ambition in my life. 'By all means,' he had replied, 'but war is now almost certain. However, if London and the School are still there after the war, you must certainly join us.' Five years later I presented myself in Canadian army uniform at the door of his home in Fulham, on the occasion of one of his famous weekly open-house sessions, and reminded him of his promise. He laughed, pretending, as I suspected, to recall our earlier conversation, and replied, 'But I said *after* the war.' 'That was understood,' I said, 'but I am just reminding you that I intend to keep you to your promise.'

In the course of my inglorious military career up to that point I had had one really good break. Through what appeared to have been an arithmetical error on the part of the military bureaucracy, the Canadian army had trained a huge surplus of artillery officers, of whom I was one. We were told we would be sent on 'conversion courses' for the infantry. (For one terrible moment I saw myself leading my men over the top with my swagger stick, as Major Attlee was said to have done in the First War); but we would have to wait months, perhaps years, before this conversion could take place. The second front had not yet been opened in Europe and it was widely assumed that it might take five to ten years before Germany and—in that pre-atomic era—Japan, in particular, could be beaten. Meanwhile it was clear that the army would be frankly relieved if we could find any sort of even quasi-military activity to occupy our time.

I managed to secure an attachment to the Wartime Information Board in Ottawa which was engaged in preparing for the Canadian forces a programme based on the Army Bureau of Current Affairs (ABCA) in Britain; I was soon posted to London, where in the course of the next two years I had an enormously interesting time. David Lewis, the National Secretary of the CCF, had put me in touch with George Strauss MP and his wife Patricia, then a war correspondent for the *New York Herald Tribune*, who have remained my close friends ever since. When they learned of my interest in British politics, they welcomed me into their own circle of friends, which included a wide variety of the lowly and the eminent, including servicemen and women, usually of Left-wing persuasion, for whom their London home was an intellectual haven. And after the formation of the Attlee Government, in which George Strauss was a minister, the Strauss household in London and their cottage in Sussex became a centre of what I am sure must have been one of the liveliest debates on the unfolding record of that Government. Aneurin Bevan and Jenny Lee were particular friends, and among junior ministers there were Hugh Gaitskell, Douglas Jay and others, with an ample representation of independent spirits like Michael Foot, George Orwell and Arthur Koestler. The experience of those years confirmed beyond all question my intention to return to London and to do my postgraduate research on some aspect of British politics at LSE.

It would be difficult to exaggerate the sense of excitement for anyone like myself, in his twenties and of social democratic persuasion, who found himself in London *and* at LSE immediately after the war. The first social democratic Government to take office with a clear majority in any major industrial democracy had just been elected at Westminster (no one paid much attention in those days to the fact that Labour in 1945 had won office with only 48 per cent of the vote). The Labour Government was committed to the introduction of what then seemed the ultimate 'cradle-to-the-grave' system of social security based on the Beveridge Report; to a comprehensive national health service which was to be completely free to those who were ill; to the abolition of unemployment on the basis of the policies devised by Keynes and popularized by Beveridge in his *Full Employment in a Free Society*; to bring into public ownership major sections of the economy; to dismantle the British Empire, beginning with the granting of Indian independence; and to conduct a foreign policy which would attempt to secure the establishment of the new world order created on the basis of the United Nations.

LSE, as I shall argue later, was not then, has never been, and is not now, in any sense a Left-wing institution, indeed if anything the reverse. The fact was, however, that a majority of the architects of what I called, in a perhaps over-enthusiastic pamphlet written during my year back in Canada, *Revolution: British Style*, were associated with the School: its founders Sidney and Beatrice Webb; Tawney, whose writings on equality had been enormously influential in the development of Labour thinking; Beveridge (Director of the School, 1919–37) who, though no socialist, was the author of two of the wartime documents on which much of Labour's domestic policy was based; Attlee, the new Prime Minister, who had taught at the School, as had Dalton, the Chancellor, a prominent figure in the teaching of economics between the wars; and Laski, the Professor of Political Science, who in 1945–46, was the highly controversial chairman of the National Executive of the Labour Party. There was therefore an inevitable sense in which the 'revolution of 1945' was seen as an invention of the London School of Economics and Political Science.

At my first meeting with Laski in his capacity as my supervisor in late September 1947, I mentioned that I had had an offer of a place at Peterhouse but, after reflection, I had decided I preferred LSE. 'That was the wisest decision you ever made,' he said. 'There is nothing going on in Cambridge of any importance in the fields in which you are interested and, as a postgraduate with the war behind you, you would be

bored by their college system.' Oxford and Cambridge, he
added, took the view that the only point in taking a second
degree is to cover up a bad first degree; indeed he doubted if
they would ever have begun awarding postgraduate degrees
if it were not to humour the Germans, Americans and Canad-
ians. No, LSE was the place for me, and we must now settle
on a first-class topic for my research. Then all I needed to do
was to get on with it. He explained what I had not quite
realized, that LSE had 'none of this American nonsense about
requiring Ph.D. candidates to write comprehensive preliminary
examinations prior to undertaking research. ... the most
soul-destroying system since the Inquisition.' What did I want
to work on? Something, I said, on the nature of political
parties and in particular, I thought, the role of the mass party.
That could not have been better, 'All of us,' he said, 'go on
saying that parties are the essence of our political system but
nobody has done an empirical study of British political parties
since Ostrogorski, a French Professor of Russian origin, who
wrote his *Democracy and the Organization of Political Parties* at the
end of the last century, an astonishing book although the
author was quite possibly mad. Read it,' he said, 'and also
Michel's *Political Parties*, written a decade or so later, with its
sociological "iron law" about the nature of oligarchy in
political parties. And that reminds me,' he added, 'you must
learn some sociology. We are the only place in the country that
teaches the subject; they do not believe it exists at Oxford and
Cambridge.' He suggested I should attend Morris Ginsberg's
lectures; and he added a remark, in what seemed almost an
afterthought, which turned out to be of critical importance to
me: 'I will propose *joint* supervision, myself and a young
assistant lecturer in Sociology called Donald MacRae; he is
astonishingly knowledgeable and will tell you what to read in
sociology.' (Laski himself was to live only two and a half years;
but my junior supervisor—a few years my own junior in age,
in fact—has remained my mentor, dear friend and colleague
for thirty years.)

As I went out the door Laski called after me, 'I would like you to be one of my teaching assistants, taking classes in connection with my introductory course on the British constitution. And why not come round to the house on Tuesday night. It's the first open-house of the term and, subject to the capacity of the living-room, all students are welcome; let my secretary know if you want to come.'

I wandered out of his office in a daze and sat down with a pint in the LSE pub, The Three Tuns. This was the Laski whom only his students knew and whom I had just met as teacher for the first time. Despite his enormous international fame, despite the outpouring of books, articles, speeches, despite his deep involvement in the politics of the Labour Party, he was more completely devoted than any university teacher I have ever known to the well-being of his students, regardless of their individual merits. He seemed to take just as much interest in the fate of the slow-witted as the high-flyer; he went to enormous trouble and very considerable personal expense to help those in difficulties; letters poured from his pen by way of introduction or to smooth the way for some student who needed help perhaps in his research, or who was looking for a job. Whenever I have felt inclined to cut corners in dealing with some particularly tedious student I recall the memory of Harold Laski and it puts me to shame.

As I began my own postgraduate research into the workings of British political parties I soon became aware of two facts of great importance. First, there was an enormous body of primary source material, such as the literature published by the parties themselves, verbatim conference reports and so forth, which had never been used for academic purposes. And second, that no previous academic researcher, as far as I could discover, had ever made use of even the most rudimentary methods of participant-observation, such as attending the party conferences, sitting in on local party meetings, observing MPs at work in their 'surgeries', canvassing and so forth.

So with the warm encouragement of Laski and MacRae I

began moving simultaneously on all fronts, quite oblivious of the strong probability that I might become swamped by my materials, as in fact I soon was. In my magpie zeal I began collecting a mountain of documentary material. It was in the days before the Xerox machine and since I did not type I could see no alternative but to hire a high-speed shorthand typist to work by my side for many months copying out passages from party documents and other sources which I had to use in the party libraries. But how was this to be financed? I had no research funds (I was supported by a British Council grant and had £14 a month from the Canadian Department of Veterans' Affairs as a result of my service with the Canadian army, but these sources ran out after two years). Then, in 1949 with the encouragement of Laski and MacRae I applied for a post to which I was subsequently appointed, as assistant-lecturer in the Department of Sociology, where I was to work with Donald MacRae on the development of political sociology, a subject not then taught at any British university. But this brought me only £550 a year, a salary which did not increase over the next four years. The answer, I decided, was to get some sort of free-lance outside employment which would enable me to finance my research. Here my early experience in radio broadcasting stood me in good stead; I had been employed for three months by the Canadian Broadcasting Corporation, awaiting my induction into the army, when I helped to set up a series of weekly programmes for the CBC radio network on the problems of the post-war world.

The London office of the CBC agreed to give me employment as a 'stringer' (occasional broadcaster) on British politics. This connection also enabled me to get press credentials for attendance at party conferences and many other big political occasions. On some such exercise I met Howard K. Smith who had recently succeeded the legendary Edward R. Murrow as the London correspondent of the Columbia Broadcasting System of the United States. I had read and much admired Smith's *Last Train from Berlin* and found him perhaps the most intellectually stimulating broadcast-journalist I had ever met. I mentioned my free-lance work for CBC and to my great surprise he asked me if I would like to do similar occasional work for CBS. So perhaps once a month I found myself doing $1\frac{1}{2}$ minute commentaries on some aspect of British politics for transmission on the CBS morning show networked across America. From my point of view this was now an ideal arrangement. I had the status of 'working journalist' which got me into press conferences and occasional interviews with prominent politicians which I would have been unable to obtain otherwise. And the profit I made I proceeded to plough straight back into my research.

It was one of the great joys of LSE, more taken advantage of by my generation of ex-service postgraduate students than by the ordinary peace-time intake, that we could so relatively easily try our wings in journalism, broadcasting or for that matter in practical politics. One of my best LSE friends of those years, who also did work as a stringer for CBS, was Paul Niven; he went on to become one of the top political broadcast-journalists of his day in the United States before his desperately premature death in a fire in the early 1960s. Another particular friend among the American postgraduates, who also dabbled in journalism and politics while a postgraduate student, was Daniel Patrick Moynihan, now Democratic Senator for New York. After leaving LSE he was for a time on the staff of Averell Harriman when he was Governor of New York; thereafter he served first as under-secretary and subsequently with full cabinet rank under no less than four presidents, Kennedy, Johnson, Nixon and Ford. In between these appointments he managed to hold a chair at Harvard, to write three or four important books, and to serve as American Ambassador first to India and then to the United Nations. It would be an exaggeration to say that I foresaw this sort of future for Pat Moynihan when we were postgraduate students together at LSE; but he was a marvellously vivacious companion from whom ideas erupted like some great pyrotechnic display. When I attended a reception in his honour in Washington at the beginning of January 1977, following his swearing-in as a member of the Senate, I remarked to one of his aides that Pat was LSE's second Senator (the other being John Towers of Texas who had been a member of my seminar on political parties while at the School). 'Very appropriate,' replied the aide, 'two Senators from each State and two from LSE.'

It will be clear from what I have written that from almost my first days at LSE I established a pattern which has persisted for 30 years since. As a student and teacher of political sociology, with a particular interest in political behaviour and such related matters as the problems of power, of political communication and so forth, I have found it of inestimable value to involve myself in at least one aspect of the real world of politics, through broadcasting. During these thirty years I have interviewed, or taken part in discussions with every British Prime Minister since Churchill, as well as with scores of cabinet ministers who served under them. Among foreign leaders I have taken part in broadcasts with Richard Nixon, Indira Gandhi, Golda Meir, Colonel Nasser, Kwame Nkrumah, Willy Brandt, Lester Pearson and Pierre Trudeau (who was also a postgraduate student with me at LSE after the war). The most rewarding experience of all was recording some 15 hours of personal reflections on politics with Harold Macmillan. I have read somewhere the suggestion that the only laymen who ever met the Renaissance princes were the portrait painters who attended their courts; and there is a sense in which their contemporary equivalents are the television interviewers. Among those I am, I suppose, one of the few who has combined an academic interest in the study of political behaviour with the personal opportunity to take part in the process of political communication through the mass media. I like to hope that both my teaching and research have benefited from this cross-fertilizing process.

But to return to the saga of my postgraduate research: I felt myself on the point of being totally submerged by my data.

I had helped to devise yet another source of primary, or at least first-hand, material for my understanding of how political parties actually operate. And this was also to contribute to the *embarras de richesse*. When I joined the full-time staff of the School, Donald MacRae and I launched a postgraduate seminar on political parties (MacRae's place was later taken by Richard Pear). Part of the work of the seminar was done by the postgraduate students themselves, reviewing and discussing the relevant literature on political parties. Rather more than half of the seminar sessions were taken up with informal discussions with politicians at every level in British political life, including leading figures of the day like Clement Attlee and Herbert Morrison, as well as second rank figures some of whom were later to reach the top. Here we can claim to have singled out a junior Tory whip, Edward Heath, who was so impressive in his explanation of the inner workings of the Tory party in Parliament that we had him back a second year running. Harold Wilson, then in the wilderness following his resignation from the Attlee Cabinet in 1951, also visited the seminar. He described in fascinating detail the internal struggles within the Labour Party following his resignation along with Aneurin Bevan and John Freeman; in thanking him I remarked that if he ever grew tired of his Byzantine life in the Labour Party we would always welcome him back to the groves of academe. 'Oh not that,' Mr Wilson remarked, 'parliamentary intrigue is absolutely nothing compared to what goes on in any senior common room.' We also brought into the seminar speakers from the party central offices, local party agents and individual party activists. So far as I am aware this was the first time at any British university that practising politicians from every branch of the party organizations were invited, on a systematic basis, to take part in a postgraduate seminar on the study of political behaviour.

After I had been pursuing my research project for perhaps three or four years Donald MacRae quite properly warned me that this process could become a never-ending one, and he strongly enjoined me to call a halt in the assembly of data and 'for God's sake to get something down on paper', if only to convince the School authorities that I was in fact engaged in a serious research project. By now, however, another problem had emerged. Following the death of Laski in early 1950 my senior supervisor had become Professor William Robson; our personal relations were amicable enough but I sensed as I began developing my ideas about the Labour Party, and in particular the argument that its internal mechanisms bore no relationship to its own theories about itself, that I was going to have some difficulty convincing Robson, himself a long-standing Labour Party supporter, that I was on the right track. As I explained this gloomily to MacRae he said, 'Well, there's a much better alternative. Why not simply write a book and forget the idea of completing a Ph.D. thesis?'

The draft material which I had so far written amounted to perhaps one quarter of the probable length of the full manuscript; but through MacRae's good offices the material was submitted to Heinemann the publishers for consideration. They readily offered me a contract, although they warned me that there was a rumour of another book which might soon appear in the field (this I suspect is a well-established ruse on the part of publishers who are suspicious of the capacity of authors to complete a manuscript in time). In any event, the ploy worked and I began a daily crash action programme of dictating and writing in the winter of 1953–54 with the help of my privately-employed part-time stenographer. Heinemann produced the bound page proof of a six-hundred page book entitled *British Political Parties* at amazing speed in the summer of '54. Suddenly the idea emerged from somewhere that it might be 'just worth picking up the Ph.D. en route' and I asked MacRae whether he knew of anything in the regulations of the University of London that precluded my presenting the bound page proofs of a book in lieu of the usual type-written thesis. It appeared there was not and he egged me on in this rather audacious exercise. The external examiner at my oral,

Professor Dennis Brogan, was much amused by this and remarked that at least it would save the examining committee the necessity of answering the traditional question on the Ph.D. candidate's report form: is the thesis worthy of publication? The degree was duly awarded, and when the thesis was published in book form in January 1955 Alan Hill of Heinemann, one of the most inventive of publishers, decided to throw a launching party to which were invited the politicians who had contributed to the exercise through appearances at the seminar or in other ways. Almost all of them, headed by Attlee, accepted, and it proved a most satisfactory launch. Thus ended my postgraduate research at LSE; I doubt whether it could have happened in just this way at any other academic institution.

I should like to conclude with some general observations on the School as I have known it over the past thirty years. First, I never cease to be amazed by LSE's long-standing reputation as, in some sense, a Left-wing institution. This originally arose no doubt from the role played by the Webbs in its foundation. But few seem to be aware of Sidney's own conception of the School. In recalling his role in its foundation, he wrote in 1903 that he himself was 'a person of decided views, Radical and socialist' and that he wanted the policy he believed in to prevail. But he was also 'a profound believer in knowledge and science and truth'. And he thought that the country was suffering much from lack of research in social matters which he was eager to promote. 'I believed,' he wrote, 'that research and new discoveries would prove some, at any rate, of my views of policy to be right, but that, if they proved the contrary I should count it all the more gain to have prevented error, and should cheerfully abandon my own policy.' (Would that Webb's view prevailed more widely today, particularly among the student Left.)

In fact, the School has been in my experience an essentially conservative institution in almost every sense of the term. To take first the political orientation of its staff: in the nine post-war elections, during all of which I have been a member of the Senior Common Room, I have no doubt that the senior staff at least have voted to the right of the nation. In addition, the School has been conservative—compared with comparable institutions elsewhere—in its attitudes to such academic matters as curricula (including inter-disciplinary studies), methods of teaching and of student assessment. LSE was also conservative in its response to the initial student demands in the 1960s for participation in the government of the college, although the School did subsequently fall in line with common practice elsewhere. I am not attempting to re-open the debate on any of these issues; arguably the conservatives and tradi-tionalists have been right and the radicals and reformers wrong. But that the School's collective position on these matters is essen-tially conservative does not seem to me to be open to dispute.

There is, however, one aspect of the School's conservatism which I have found a cause for concern: what I feel is the too limited involvement of the staff in the making of public policy in this country. I must make it clear that I am fully aware of the enormously important links between particular members of staff and the Whitehall departments, industry, the heads of trade unions, and so on; but even the senior teachers of the School—with a few notable exceptions—have seemed to me curiously uninvolved both in party political activity on the one hand and in the great public debate which has welled up in recent decades on the problems of British society, on the other.

In trying to account for this, three considerations have occurred to me. First was the reaction to Beveridge, Director of the School for almost the whole of the inter-war period, who had been of course tremendously involved in public debate about major issues in British society. Despite his great personal qualities he was a domineering Director, a powerful egoist, eager to maximize his public influence by almost any means. When Beveridge parted company with the School, denouncing the economists, and also by clear implication Harold Laski, in his final address, it was evident that a powerful reaction against his type of domineering Director would set in. Over the next thirty-five years the School, half-deliberately, half-unconsciously, chose for itself a series of three Directors (Sir Alexander Carr-Saunders 1937–57; Sir Sydney Caine 1957–67; and Sir Walter Adams 1967–74) who, both by temperament and the nature of their personal interests, were most unlikely to take part in debates over public policy (nor, of course, would they provoke within the School the bitterness and hostility aroused by Beveridge). All of these Directors were, in their different ways, devoted servants of the School; but only Carr-Saunders was a scholar of repute in his own right, and like the others he did not seem much interested in promoting the School's public role in the making of public policy.

The second consideration, related in some respects to the first, was the School's attempt—again I think half-conscious—to exorcise what might be called the 'Laski factor' in its reputation. It is probably true to say that in the 'thirties, and until the sad decline in Laski's public standing set in after 1945, he got more publicity abroad and perhaps in this country than all the other members of staff put together. The School authorities had been deeply pained by this and in 1934 Beveridge referred the problem to what was then known as the Emergency Committee of the School. They passed a resolution declaring that 'the development of public opinion concerning Professor Laski's recent more popular utterances is, in fact, rightly or wrongly against the best interests of the School and ought now be taken by him into account in deciding on [his] "personal duty" [under a Professorial Council Resolution passed in 1931].' There could be no doubt that Laski's reputation as perhaps the leading socialist intellectual in the democratic world was tending to refurbish the School's wholly misleading reputation as a hotbed of socialism.

The reaction to Laski took various forms, the first of which was the choice of his successor, Michael Oakeshott, an unobtrusive but very distinguished philosophical conservative. I remember, at the beginning of the great debate over British

entry into the Common Market in the early 1960s, being
surprised that Oakeshott had agreed to chair a public lecture
at the School on this subject. At the dinner for the guest speaker
afterward I asked Michael where he stood personally on the
issue of British entry. He, the head of political studies at the
LSE, replied, 'I do not find it necessary to hold opinions on such
matters.'

I think the attempt to exorcise the Laski influence was a
factor in other appointments in addition to Oakeshott's. A. J. P.
Taylor, to take but one example, applied some years ago, I
understand, for a chair at the School but was passed over in
favour of a very competent but much duller rival. Although
Taylor is a very different animal from Laski, he is in certain
respects squarely in the Laski tradition, in no way hesitant
about promoting his political and other opinions. I am not
for a moment suggesting there is any element of political
bias in these or other cases; I have no doubt the committee
chose A. N. Other over Taylor solely on the basis of his
superior academic merits, but I feel for several decades after
Laski's death there was a largely unconscious tendency, other
things being equal, to prefer appointees who would not revive
the 'Laski tradition'.

This brings me to the view, which I believe to be widely
held in the School, that party political activity—of whatever
persuasion, of the Left or of the Right—is somehow unworthy
of the true academic. In his autobiography, which is essential
reading for anyone who would understand the School, Lord
Robbins remarks that it was sometimes hinted that after his
wartime service in the cabinet offices he remained a sort of
'*éminence grise* beyond the scenes, advising the Treasury and
influencing ministers, especially Conservative ministers, concerning the principles of policy'. This view, Robbins tells us
emphatically, is 'baseless'; he was consulted only twice in the
fifteen-year period 1946–61. Since departing the cabinet offices,
Robbins writes, he 'scrupulously avoided any attempt to
obtrude [his] opinions on [his] late colleagues or on ministers'.

Yet Robbins's autobiography bristles with criticisms, many of them obviously justified, of the economic policies and of the follies and disasters perpetrated, usually with the best of motives, by successive British Governments in this period. I would have been more impressed if Lord Robbins had told us that he had used the private dining-room at LSE, which after all is located twenty minutes from Westminster, as a forum in which ministers and MPs particularly concerned with economic questions regularly met to exchange ideas with Lord Robbins himself and the brightest sparks in the Economics Department at LSE.

I would go further: in my view the members of the School ought to be encouraged by their seniors to get involved in the policy-making procedures of the political parties themselves. Labour in particular sees its party manifesto, in Richard Crossman's phrase, as 'the battering ram of change' (and that was not far from Mr Heath's attitude when he took office in 1970). Why should the process of policy-making, particularly when a party is in opposition, be left primarily to the active politicians supported by their officials in the party's central office? Why should not the leading figures and the bright juniors of a School like LSE be positively encouraged to become deeply involved in the formulation of party programmes and policies of the political parties of their preference? I find it baffling and disappointing that the staff of great American institutions like Harvard should be so much more intimately involved in both governmental and party political activity in their own country.

Mercifully, I think the attitude of the School has changed very considerably in the last few years since the appointment of Ralf Dahrendorf as Director in October 1974. He himself is the first Director since Beveridge to be a public figure of great distinction (I recently suggested to an Anglo-German audience that he was already the most influential German in Britain since Prince Albert), and there is no doubt of his concern to ensure that members of the School should be deeply involved in the process of developing public policy.

I hope it will be clear from what I have written that I have the profoundest regard and affection for LSE; my association with it for more than thirty years has been the great central experience of my life. For various reasons I think it is a less intellectually exciting place that it was in the late 'thirties, or in the great moment of change just after the Second World War. But all these judgements are comparative and I would not hesitate to say that today, for the student in the social sciences, the School, with its great library, its distinguished staff and its location, is still probably the most interesting place in the world to study. I find in my travels that graduates of the School constitute a world-wide fraternity. When I was attending a conference in Japan last year a Japanese economist spoke to me saying how sorry he was that I had not let the LSE Society of Tokyo know of my arrival. They had, he explained, a thriving branch of 300 members and would have been delighted to arrange a meeting with me. To study at the School is, to a remarkable degree, to acquire a lifetime commitment to it.

Postscript: Sex at LSE

Since the topic looms so large in many of the essays in *My Oxford* and *My Cambridge* I feel I would be letting the side down if I did not make some reference to sex at LSE. I was startled to learn from John Mortimer's chapter in *My Oxford* what a large proportion of his waking hours, and of those of his undergraduate contemporaries, was spent in trying to find an escape route from schoolboy homosexuality into adult heterosexuality. He had been at Oxford both early in the war and immediately after the war and he remarked that it was only in post-war Oxford 'that heterosexuality came to be completely tolerated'. I hope it will not prove disappointing if I say I cannot remember a single conversation with any of my contemporaries at LSE which was devoted to these or related themes. This does not mean that I accept the charge sometimes levelled against LSE that it is an essentially sexless place. It acquired this bogus reputation in part, I think, because of the reputation of its founders, the Webbs. They have been described as 'two typewriters typing as one', and Beatrice is on record as saying that 'marriage [and I suspect she would have included all sexual relations] is the waste-basket of the emotions'. But in my days as a student at LSE sex was certainly not viewed with Beatrice's puritan scorn; as I recall, sex was taken for granted as a perfectly natural concomitant of a full life, much as it is by students today. We were simply ahead of our time. I remember one of my con-temporaries describing an effort made by the then warden of the School's hostel for men students to impose certain rules about entertaining women guests in one's rooms; this produced a revolt leading to a firm decision by the student council that the only rule they would tolerate was that one did not bring one's female guest to breakfast.

On reflection I *can* recall one conversation about sex, initiated by an Australian postgraduate who had missed the war. In the course of a heavy session of beer in The Three Tuns he declared that he had no intention of leaving the 'fleshpots of Europe' and returning to the family ranch in the Australian outback, until he had 'experimented with every form of sexual activity known to man'. All he had managed in life so far, before he left Australia, he confessed, apart from 'laying his (girl) cousin', was 'a little bestiality'. The young calves, he said, 'as any farm boy knows, can easily be taught fellatio'. We began compiling for him a list of sexual activities we had gleaned, largely, I suspect, from our reading of Kraft Ebbing and de Sade. The Australian did not quail until we reached coprophilia and necrophilia, which he rejected 'on aesthetic grounds'. He did however issue a challenge: would we join him that night on an expedition into Soho to see how far we could get through the list we had compiled? We agreed. I can well remember the four of us setting out by taxi from The Three Tuns, but I cannot for the life of me remember how the evening ended.

Ron Moody

Ron Moody attended the LSE from 1948–53, and it was while he was there studying Sociology that he 'stumbled' into his acting career. Peter Myers and Ronnie Cass offered him a part in one of their intimate revues at the New Lindsey Theatre, from where he went straight into the West End in Intimacy at 8.30, For Amusement Only and For Adults Only. He became an international star through his creation of the role of Fagin in both the stage and film versions of Oliver!, a part which won him a nomination for an Oscar, and five international best actor awards, including the Hollywood Golden Globe and the Moscow Golden Bear. Other film credits include The Twelve Chairs with Mel Brooks, Summer Holiday and The Flight of the Doves with Ralph Nelson. He has made countless television appearances (including 'Starsky and Hutch' and plays by Bernard Kops), and his numerous British stage appearances include Hamlet at the Globe Playhouse, Bankside, pantomime, and a highly successful one-man show, Move Along Sideways, which he played to rave reviews for four seasons at the Theatre Royal, Stratford. He is now working on his fifth musical, in between playing the pubs and clubs from Bethnal Green to Bombay.

'**O**h, no! No, no, no! Absolutely impossible!'

The Squadron Leader S.Ad.O. was against me at once, even before he'd seen me. Which he never actually did, because from the moment I entered, his eyes had been fixed on the second button of my tunic.

'Oh, no, no, no! I can't see how you can possibly have full time off!' (Nor could I, but I was hopeful.) 'At this—er— London School of Economics?' He thought about it for a moment, and made himself very angry. I could tell because his eyes moved up to my first button. It occurred to me that if I provoked him enough, he might actually look me in the eye.

'I'll let you know about it!'

'Sir!'

I left without rancour because it was clear that this happy little haberdasher had never even heard of LSE. The Education Officer had, but he hadn't known what to suggest so he had referred me to the Squadron Leader. That same afternoon I was referred to the Commanding Officer (superior type— eyes on badge of hat) who couldn't give me full time off, but would see what the Education Officer had to suggest. After two trips round this Inner Circle somebody decided I could have some time off, but I must arrange my studies to take up as little RAF time as possible. So I spent my first term at LSE as an evening student.

It would have been much simpler if I'd been demobbed in time for the Michaelmas Term in October 1947, but the course of true life never runs smooth. So I spent my days in the Radar section at Hendon, doing DI's on Ansons, poodling around with Lucero and IIC, toying with impedances and rejector circuits, and cursing clots who switched the RX so the gain was duff; and my evenings at LSE, listening to Robbins on Indifference curves, Blackburn on hyperaesthesia, Hinchliff on the Bhuddist Dhammapada, and wondering why the hell the lecturers couldn't speak plain English.

I moved from jargon to jargon, milieu to milieu, a marginal man on the fringe of two worlds, blurring together like an off-phase projector. I lived for the evenings, and, paradoxically, had more fun with the days. The Radar section had Ken and Dave, who were my close friends, LSE was a passing show of anonymous strangers; the RAF provided me with crosswords, NAAFI breaks, table tennis and the radio-set I never did build, LSE gave me wallflower evenings at Freshers' Dances, Union Meetings where I sat in awe as 'giants' spake, and a delicately nurtured inferiority complex. It was in the RAF that I saw a Jamaican bash a cook over the head with a vinegar bottle because he was refused more potatoes. LSE yielded no such happy moments.

Unless perhaps that cold October Sunday when I joined the LSE Boat Club and paddled out from Chiswick Boathouse in my first four. Eight arms and four oars punched the boat through the water at terrifying speed, I caught a crab, the boat heeled to one side, the oar thudded my ribs, and the purpose of the sport became alarmingly clear—to get back to the bank! As we did, I saw a lone rower, swimming towards us like a drowned rat, pushing his upturned shell before him—and I never went again.

But I was at LSE—the only place of Higher Learning I had ever wanted to be! I was a guest in the house of Bernard Shaw and the Webbs, the Citadel where Laski held court. And above all, I was a University Student! Part Time!

'Number, Rank, Name!'
  '1894342, AC1, Moody, R., Corporal!'
  'Age!'
  '24, Corporal!'
  'Sign that . . . that . . . that . . . that!'
  'What's the date, Corporal?
  '12th January, 1948! It's yer demob day—twit!'
  'Now come on, chaps!' A Flight Lieutenant with an insensitivity of cosmic proportions joshed us affectionately. 'Take your demob leave, chaps, then remember the old esprit de corps, chaps, and come back with the boys, chaps.'
  We took our eyes from the top button of his tunic and plunged through a series of corridors and offices and hangers in a never-ending stream, picking up money and chits and sports jackets and pin-striped trousers, and seeing—oh, blessed moment!—our Release Books ripped and torn to pieces before our bewildered eyes. Free. Free! Oh, madness and joy! Freeeeeeee!

On January 14th, 1948, a magnificent new Birthday Briefcase from Proud and Happy Parents gleaming in my Proud and Happy Hand, I set off for LSE to begin my new life as a University Student! Full Time!
  Part time, full time, in no time at all I was Alice in Wonderland! Wandering through warrens of classes and lectures and societies and seminars. . . . Ah! There was the Dormouse, pretending to be Professor Ginsberg, there, the White Rabbit, disguised thinly as Lionel Robbins, and as for the Mad Hatter, why, he was everywhere, proliferating himself onto every lecture platform in the place, pouring out platitudes of garbled logic and gobbledegook to the wisely nodding heads of Them What Was In The Know—everyone, that is—except me.
  And of course, there were thousands of Cheshire Cats, smiling widely from afar and fading mysteriously when I came too close. When I discovered that if I kept very quiet, the Cheshire Cats would allow me to approach and listen to their

conversations, I became an excellent listener, a master of the
role of attentive audience. But if I was foolish enough to open
my mouth and say one word, they would fade instantly about
their business.

I lost the power of speech. The outrageous exhibitionist of
the RAF, the buffoon of every barrack room, the Aneurin Bevan
of every NAAFI from Hendon to Henlow. I was suddenly struck
dumb! My syntax went to pieces and my sentences tailed off
in mid-air. I was too busy listening to my own, thin, nasal
voice, my own vulgar London accent, so damnably aware that
everybody else spoke so *well*! I went to a public-speaking class,
determined to cure my disability, the Cheshire Cats orated—
and I listened. When I was finally forced to speak, the trapped
Cheshires listened back—and stopped smiling.

It was about this time that I developed my Nod, a symbol of
acquiescence in group discussion, the limit of my participation
in group activity. It carried me through classes, lectures, Union
meetings and Refectory debates with considerable dignity. I
became a Wise Silent Nodder Who Understood All. For of
course, I did! I was intensely critical of Robbins and Marshall
and Ginsberg and Hinchliff and Beales and Smellie, who con-
tinuously missed the points that were so laughably clear to me,
and without having had to read any of their recommended
books! For was I not already a Shavian Creative Evolutionist,
a Radical Socialist, a Rationalist and a Very Clever Person to
boot? I was overcome with admiration for the student at a
Robbins lecture on Economic Analysis, who, when that
learned Prof. warned us that the lecture would be sticky if we
hadn't read Marshall, stood up, bowed, and walked out.
Almost as good as the Jamaican and the vinegar bottle. The
only lecturer I really approved of was Dr Mannheim, who
introduced us to the heinous realities of Criminology and
earned himself my affectionate title of 'Homicidal Hermann'.

I would probably have nodded my way through the next
two years at LSE with no trouble, no loss of face and no degree,
if I hadn't, one morning in February, taken my FIRST BIG

STEP! I replied to an advertisement for the post of cartoonist on *Beaver*, the wall newspaper in The Three Tuns. Cartoons and cruel caricatures had been a happy hobby since childhood—I revelled in long noses, buck teeth and piggy eyes and drew and lost many friends in the process. A few days later I found a letter in my pigeon-hole from 'Tiger' Standish, the Editor, to say my application was gratefully accepted and would I cover the Valentine Ball? Fee, a free 4/6d ticket! The offer was irresistible! I had a Government grant of £180 per annum, lived at home and gave a pound a week to my very dear parents, and managed my LSE on two pounds a week. I covered the Ball, with cartoons and comments on the types and personalities present—LSE came out of it as the only college where all the men had bow legs and all the women had flat chests—and had the enormous pleasure of nipping down to The Three Tuns one lunchtime to find my piece prominently displayed on the *Beaver* notice-board—and surrounded by a swarm of flat-chested, bow-legged students. I had signed it, unobtrusively, 'Juma Krash', and I skulked around for a few changes of audience, revelling in the joy I brought to their piggy eyes and reading it a few dozen times myself. 'Brilliant!' the Walrus said; 'Very very funny,' returned the Carpenter. I nodded.

From that day, I had (you should excuse the expression) function and status. I was 'Juma Krash', the unobtrusive *Beaver* cartoonist and if you were nice to me I could put your face on my wall. I began to spend my spare time in the *Beaver* office and suddenly found myself in growing contact with the student élite—for the Union office was on the third floor. It wasn't long before I was asked to illustrate an article in *Clare Market Review*, the *printed* student periodical, edited by Val Sherman, iconoclast elect, egotist supreme, and already a brilliant journalist. I viewed him with some awe because he used to stand up with great authority at climactic moments in the Union meetings—and speak! And he had made up his mind that I was a budding Daumier and was wasting my time reading Sociology and should be a political cartoonist on a national newspaper. How could I possibly consider such an idea? I was devoted to the ideal of an academic life. I attended every lecture on the syllabus, took copious notes in my meticulously organized, precisely tabulated master file, and one day soon, I would read them all and understand them and assimilate them—if I could decipher them.

Like Mr Lewisham, I had a schedule of work, a plan of study. For a start, I got up every morning. It was never easy, now I was free of RAF discipline—perhaps I went to bed too late. It would have to stop! I *must* keep to my schedule, ten minutes of push-ups and exercises, half an hour of German translation before breakfast! No time now, but I would have to begin tomorrow! Definitely and absolutely, tomorrow! I rushed breakfast, took the tube to Holborn, jog-trotted along Kingsway, making small but significant gestures as I passed the RAF Recruiting HQ, all the time cursing my ineptitude and my idiotic, inexcusable unpunctuality! Late every morning! Late again for Robbins in the New Theatre, scribble, scribble, what *was* he on about, egad, the man was so tall, no wonder he talked above our heads, hahaha! Stigler! That was the answer! I must read Stigler's *Theory of Price* and all would be revealed— tomorrow! Definitely and absolutely tomorrow! No time now, I had to illustrate *Beaver* Hansard for Tiger and discuss drawings for *CMR* with Val. Anyway the Easter vacation was upon us, and I would now positively get down to some real work on all subjects. Definitely and absolutely!

In fact, I went to the NUS Congress at Leicester as an observer (subsidized) for *CMR*, and had my first taste of life in a student hostel, an old country house with huge grounds, oak panelling and no ghosts—nodding sagely through lectures by Dr Joad and Arthur Horner, listening with satisfaction to the inanities of their student critics, going to endless socials and informal hops, walking girls home halfway across the county, then walking back so late I had to climb in through the hostel window— this was *living*!—and finding some of the old RAF companionship with Len Hiscock, the Landsberger twins and students from other colleges. I hated to leave and go back to London. For the first time I felt I really belonged. I had become (you should excuse the expression) integrated. The rest of the vacation was a terrible anticlimax and as soon as I had finished my strip cartoon reports on the Congress, I went into LSE. None of the warmth and bustle of term-time, but it felt good to be back. And I took my SECOND BIG STEP! I discovered the library!

I had dropped in a few times in the Lent Term, braving the caustic surveillance of the Guardians at the Gate, who, brothers to Customs men and traffic wardens, always made you feel you had half the library stuffed up your jumper. I had a paper to write on Veblen and took out his superb *Theory of the Leisure Class*. And all at once, I realized I had been wasting my time only attending lectures last term. Here were all the words, written *down*, not flying blind over my head and being humped, half-heard, into my note-book. I was able to sit and read and study and read again and think and look at other readers and admire their legs and wonder what they were reading and read what I was reading and slowly, very slowly I was able—to learn!

To the half-trained mind, the first major text book you read is close to Holy Writ—the tight-knit arguments, the force of the intellect behind them, these are over-powering and un-assailable. It is not surprising that the Bible and Marx have had such power over the Peasant. The second book fills you with helpless panic, you blunder in circles of conflicting logic like a chicken without a head. In addition to the Wise Nod, I now acquired the Blank Stare into Space. Where do these great minds differ? At what point in this jungle of juxta-positions and jargon, this plethora of paradox and premiss, do you discern the definite difference? So you begin to read books *about* the books, critical surveys, analytic assessments, flirting with Philosophy and Scientific Method, and slowly—very slowly—beginning—just beginning—to learn—*how* to learn.

THE RAGGED SCHOOL IN CLARE MARKET

In the Summer Term of 1948, my LSE was a new place. Instead of a grind of disjointed lectures with nothing in between, I now evolved a real scheme of continuous study in the library, popping out only occasionally for lectures and food, and crawling out late in the evening, stiff, smug and satiated.

On Monday, May 3rd, I read my first paper. A critique of Veblen for Miss Hinchliff's Sociology Class. With a thundering heart, a dry mouth, and a voice that had yet to learn about resonant cavities and simple articulation, Veblen never had a chance. Filled with shame and despair at my stupid inadequacy, I stumbled out, seeking fresh air and inspiration from Lincoln's Inn Fields and the Soap Box Orators. There is an old water fountain near the Law Courts—on one side the Conservatives used to damn the Labour Party and themselves into the bargain; on the other, a small dark man, with a peculiarly grating voice, would attack middle-class morality with shocking abandon and his own particular brand of socialism. I called him Jolson and became an ardent fan. I learnt from him that you may speak the most arrant nonsense or the most inspired sense, you may have the cadences of a docker or a duke—but without the power and confidence to punch it across, you embarrass the audience and yourself. So obvious—so simple—but I could not—dared not—*do* it!

Apart from this, it was a good Summer Term. My work on *Beaver* and *CMR* went from line to half-tone, I was promoted to Art Editor on both periodicals, and a rumour went round that I had worked on animation for Disney. In fact, my only link with the film business was my father, who was a construction head at Elstree Studios. But by the end of my first year at LSE, I was happily settled in, with a sense of freedom I had never known before, and two possible careers ahead of me —political cartoonist or social scientist. The Cold War was hotting up and the blockade of Berlin had begun. Freed from the common enemy, the former allies were looking to their ideological differences instead of to their mutual interests. A new war threatened the peace of the world, but LSE was a buffer against the grim reality outside, my deep sentimental attachment to the buildings and rooms and students gave me a self-contained and complete way of life. Vacations were gaps to be wished away, never enjoyed, and that summer vacation was no exception. I wished it quickly away and was back for my second year in October 1949, bursting with determination to work as I had never worked before—this term, full out— hard at it—particularly in Economics! I must read Stigler— definitely and absolutely!

If Marx had cast a long shadow in the corridors of world power, Plato and Aristotle were no less evident in the intellectual corridors of LSE. I was now able, vaguely but unwillingly, to realize that the academic world, far from being a joyous agglomeration of sincere minds seeking truth, was in fact the scene of endless cold wars of its own, thought to the finish with bewildering ferocity and intolerance. Plato vs Aristotle, Deductive vs Inductive, Theories and Methods vs Methods and Theories. There was rivalry between methodologists, between disciplines, between schools of thought within those disciplines, not to mention breakaways within those schools of thought, that manifested all the capriciousness of a dogma in the manger. For emotional and probably ethnic reasons, I favoured the Deductive method. When Ginsberg lectured on Theories and Methods of Sociology, with his beautiful, quiet understatement and lucid, gentle delivery, I sat and adored him. He would pull great big satisfying plums from his philosophical hat, reconciling the differences between Freudian and General Psychology in one lecture, then, like a small boy disobeying an order, be almost apologetic in criticizing the Marxist Theory of Knowledge.

On the other hand, there was the 'empirically oriented' Edward Shils and his Sociology Class. This astonishing little American made his debut by breezing into the room, asking us to introduce ourselves to each other with a few words about our intentions in the field of Sociology, and then proceeding to tear us apart with clipped, well-chosen epithets, delivered between clenched teeth. He was a Socrates, directing his venom against students rather than sophists. He terrified me. I liked him enormously. Probably because he once told me I had a 'certain intellectual adventurousness'. But when I once dared to Nod Wisely at one of his discourses on Modern Social Structures, he asked me to tell the class why I agreed with him! I didn't know! I didn't even know I'd Nodded. I reassured myself with the notion that the fault lay in his high level of abstraction and not in my ineptitude—but I didn't Nod within sight of him again.

I revelled in Dr Popper's 'Scientific Method' which did more to put my ideas into perspective than any other. And I began to reassess the lecturers that I had once found an infuriating waste of time. For I could dimly see that I was rising—with the inevitability of gradualness—to that primitive intellectual level that made their intellects intelligible to me. And I could dimly see that the more I journeyed in the mind, the less I would be able to communicate, eventually, with people who hadn't come along for the same ride.

I dabbled in Aesthetics and read books on the History of Art. To tie this in with my main studies, I read all I could on the Psychology of Laughter and made an analysis of newspaper cartoons to classify the type of joke and the form of the ludicrous involved. I actually began to send some of my cartoons to Fleet Street and was quite proud of my collection of Rejection Slips. For however much these efforts hovered between hobby and blocked vocation, the academic life was still my cherished goal, the university was my place. Still I dreamed that one day, from its Ivory Towers, I would shoot flaming barbs to burn down the Pallisades of Myth and Prejudice that protect the Infidel, Reaction, and bar the Believer, Progress!

I had overlooked the Dissembler, Destiny! For Forces were at work of which I had no awareness, and they were just about to put their Two Bits into the Game. It was the Summer Term, 1949.

Ken Willy Watkins, Union demagogue—oh, what a speaker *he* was—started it. He suddenly decided I should stand for Union Council! Me? Speak at Union meetings? Impossible! With Finals in 1950, not that far off? Impractical! Treating his sponsorship in the manner I felt it deserved, I drew a cartoon body with two necks, upon which I stuck two Polyphoto heads, and stuck this monstrosity on the board for Council nominations. That was that! Next day, I was handed the Council Office key by Val Schur. I had been elected by 201 votes out of 230! And I am proud to say that in my period of office, as Chairman of the Refectory Committee (which led me, naturally enough to a study of the Manual of Nutrition and a book on Physiology) I did not speak once! Not, that is, until the last Union meeting of my Nodding office, where a wag stood up and asked me a long and complicated question about Refectory matters. I stood up and said, in a strong Welsh accent: 'I shouldn't be at all surprised, actually!'

But once elected, the chain reaction was set in motion. I moved up from *Beaver* office to the Union office, where the members spent their days playing liar dice and plotting lunatic coups. One of them was Allan Kingsbury, Entertainments Officer. And he plotted a coup in the Michaelmas Term of 1949, a coup which he called a 'Smoking Concert'. And because I drew funny cartoons, he assumed I could write funny material. It just so happened that from the age of 16, with a guitar bought for me by my mother, who encouraged everything I ever did, I had been composing awful tunes. And in cahoots with an old friend, Maurice Bentley, I had moved on to writing parochial point numbers on the sexual proclivities of the Grange Park bourgeoisie. So I submitted a few ideas. Allan decided I should also perform in them, and I cannot remember my reaction to that at all. Except perhaps, fear? But somehow it all went ahead. The smoking concert grew into a full scale revue, and I suggested it be called 'Place Pigalle', because that summer I had made my first trip to Paris, and had still to recover from the breathless excitement, the vibrant magic, of my introduction to Montmartre, Sacré Coeur, and Pigalle! I had made a vow that one day I would grow a beard, go back to Montmartre, and paint—for the time being, I stayed clean-shaven and daubed the scenery for the show.

I was, of course, quite mad! With nine months to go before Finals, I plunged impetuously into all the time-consuming, life-involving, wildly fascinating activities that go into putting on a show. John Hutchinson and Len Freedman were to do their brilliant double act at the piano; Al Bermel, then Editor of *CMR* was to write and perform; Cyril Wiseman, a law student who should have been a concert pianist, was to compose and accompany; and Bernard Levin was to impersonate Harold Laski and compere. I first met Levin one evening, as he was walking ahead of me towards Holborn station. I caught him up and said, for no reason whatsoever: 'Did you know that Finsbury Park, spelt backwards, is Y–RUB–SNIF–KRAP?' He pointed out that KRAP–Y–RUB–SNIF might be more accurate, and I had found a fellow lunatic.

Oh, the days that followed! Casting, rehearsing, directing,

rewriting, auditioning, re-casting, elation, depression, inspiration, exhaustion—all punctuated with interminable cups
of coffee and inquests in Villiers Street. The Singing Chefs
Sextet lost two, acquired Groucho Marx disguises, and became
the Four Grouchos. And driving us on, sustaining our flagging
spirits, behind us all the way, was the faith and energy of Allan
Kingsbury, the finest natural producer I have ever met!

On November 15th, 1949, 'Place Pigalle' went on. We
under-rehearsed all day, adrenalin pumping from glands we
didn't know we had, total chaos took on some semblance of
shape, and I suddenly decided we needed a real horseshoe to
set up a gag where we threw rubber ones (made in Elstree) at
the audience. I left everything and everyone to hunt everywhere to find one—and I finally ran it to earth in an old forge,
housed in a seedy archway behind Kings Cross! Mortimer
Wheeler never had it so good!

That night, the Old Theatre was packed with stamping,
shouting students, thirsting for blood and targets for their wit!
They greeted the overture with a barrage of huzzahs and toilet
rolls! The predicted disaster was set before them! It was a
huge, unbelievable, rip-roaring, runaway hit! Hutchinson and
Freedman tore the place up, the Four Grouchos were a smash
and the horseshoe gag was a socko boff! The cheers and
laughter seemed to go on forever and probably did. And what
was most important to me, my mother and sister and father
were there and we all went home by tube, glowing over every
blissful moment.

I didn't sleep that night. I was floating a few feet above the
bed on a cushion of warmth that flowed into my stomach and
out of every nerve in my body. I had found the way to speak,
to project, to be strong in public, to sustain a flow of words in
public, to be a source of fun in public, and all by means of one
simple device. ... I did it as someone else! And when that
someone else was the greatest verbal wit of our time, and I
could speak his words and use his voice and wear his clothes
and lose myself beneath his Master's mask—in a word, when

I could really feel that I *was* Groucho Marx—then all his
power and glory passed to me. At second hand, perhaps!
Derivative? Of course. But it was the only way I could have
done it. And when a midget sits behind the wheel of an Aston
Martin and puts his tiny foot on the accelerator, God help
those who deny his right of way!

Inevitably, my LSE went through another metamorphosis.
The 'Place Pigalle' crowd basked in the glory of their success
for the rest of the term, went to an endless round of parties,
performed bits from the show at the drop of a hop ticket, anything to sustain the euphoria we had all found that night. We
did 'Pigalle' again in December and added a pantomime
sequence. This time I actually ventured on alone as Crusoe,
the Marginal Man, lost in a sea of Indifference curves and
plunking, very rubato, on his ukelele to satirical words by Al
Bermel. Still hidden, behind a mask of hair and furs, but all
alone, solo, I found a communion with the audience that was
even more exciting than before.

Val Sherman never commented on these activities—he was
still convinced he had found a new Low! And indeed, through
all this fabulously rich experience, my ambition was still
crystallizing firmly in its original direction. I must work hard
to get a First in 1950 and apply to lecture at LSE. . . . I wanted
to stay at LSE for ever! Where else could I have found such
fulfilment in every direction but in this Student City of
Opportunity?

In 1950, I began to work long hours in the library, and when
I found that sometimes distracting, I stayed at home and
worked into the early hours of the morning. At last I tackled
Economics! I read Robbins and wanted to apologize for all
the ungracious thoughts I had had when I first went to his
lectures in 1948—when I didn't see what he meant by *positive*
science or *formal* economics. I read Stigler and finally saw the
point of abstract *concepts*, self-regulating *mechanisms* and other
kinds of mental spectacles, which if not rose-tinted, were convenient ways of looking at the world.

'Moody,' I would say to myself, 'how have you managed to cope until this moment without knowing that MR equals MC, which under perfect competition also equals Price? And that MVP equals MR times MPP, which under perfect competition becomes p times MPP which equals V of MP? How *could* you?'

I literally ploughed through Talcott Parson's *Structure of Social Action*, an experience which I can only compare to a cerebral volcanic eruption, a thunderous restructuring of my tired brain to see the world as a structural-functional system of social action. Shils at last made sense! Weber, Durkheim, Pareto, the Utilitarians, all falling into place in one huge conceptual scheme. And even now I realized I was only beginning—beginning to learn—to understand why I was here at LSE! The panic set in! How ignorant I had been until this moment. How ignorant I still was! What a gargantuan task still lay ahead!

No man can tell another what university means—it is the experience itself that is the answer, the intellectual leap into the realms of informed ignorance, the maddening phrase 'we must learn to pose the questions' which so infuriates the Naive Custodians of Common Sense who want to know the *answers*.

On June 12, 1950, I take the tube for South Kensington . . . meet some of the LSE gang on the way in . . . we are all shaking with large butterflies in our stomachs . . . I've never seen so many people looking green. . . . I am in a huge room of the University Examination Halls, Imperial Institute Road. . . . I am sitting at a desk marked '12259' . . . I am looking at the exam papers . . . I am writing . . . I am putting down all the things I have been rehearsing for the last six months . . . not sure if some of them fit but I'm putting them down all the same . . . just so they'll know that I know even if they don't want to know. . . . I leave the room where a lifetime telescopes down into five written answers . . . a little dazed and disappointed because all my sweat on Stigler is wasted but for one question. . . .

On June 19, 1950, seven days later, I walked from the

Examination Halls to the tube, chatting with Len Hiscock. Only when he had gone did it hit me! The exam was over! I wandered around South Ken for something between ten minutes and an hour, feeling a most peculiar kind of sensation —I think it is called freedom—with a dash of relief, a soupçon of hope and a large helping of oblivion—for it is dangerous to think back for one instant over the questions, foolhardy and quite fatal ever to discuss the answers with other students! Just sit back, wait, and think happy thoughts.

I spent about 48 days doing just that. The happiest of the thoughts was that I no longer had £180 per annum to support me, and whatever happened next I needed to earn a living. Cartoons! I must make a determined onslaught on Fleet Street, and once established as a leading cartoonist, keep on at LSE and read for a Higher Degree. I drew them and sent them and got them all back—they didn't even try to steal any —nobody was interested. Not even Heywood, the Managing Editor of Kemsley Newspapers who had assured me that very January that I could have a promising career with the Press and should go to Art School. Other happy thoughts flooded in —the Korean War, and the threat of an atomic holocaust, Truman's rejection of Nehru's appeal for mediation with Russia, happy, happy thoughts!

On July 21, I went to LSE, for the results. No lists were up so I had tea with a chap who told me there were no Firsts in Sociology! Impossible! I went downstairs again and found a heaving mass crowding over the notice-boards. I fought my way through with a show of hysterical nonchalance, and peered wildly, with fast-blurring vision, at the IIA Section. My name was not there! I looked across—oh, how I looked across—to the other side of the tracks, the nether regions of IIB, the lowly sub-strata of the Lower Seconds. . . . Moody, Ronald, IIB.

Moody, Ronald, IIB! No professorship at LSE! No cartoons accepted! War in the air! Slam, bang, wallop, every line closed up tight! I called that day Black Friday and the summer that followed, the Black Summer.

For how could I have known that I was to spend two more years at LSE, vital, incredible years in which my aims and ambitions were to be totally transformed, and the Forces already set in motion were to push me in the direction that was probably evident to everyone but me.

I spent that summer 'wandering in a wilderness, devoid of signposts', a rather nice turn of phrase, I thought at the time, and then I was told that I could go back to LSE as a postgraduate student in the Psychology Department, if I could submit a satisfactory thesis for a Ph.D. Himmelweit and Hotopf were my advisers and it was up to me.

My LSE! Graduated and broke! And it was up to me! Without money, I took a succession of part-time jobs, Market Research interviews, research for the Acton Society Trust, part-time clerical work, sustained all the time by incredibly generous and rather bewildered parents, who must have wondered at the benefits of a university education, but never once pressed me to commit myself to a specific career.

Socially, nothing had changed. A flood of new faces poured in, Al Bermel initiated a new revue, I wrote some of it without much heart and it went on. But with Allan and Cyril graduated and departed, it was no more than a moderately successful failure. This hardly affected my mood, because I was trying to clear my mind on the thesis that would win me back my legitimate place at LSE. Steeped in Parson's American Methodology, it was not easy to communicate my ideas to the Social Psychology department. But Himmelweit and Hotopf were sympathetic and gave me time and eventually I became more specific and chose the field of Industrial Relations, an area where one is concerned with the interdependence of productivity and human happiness. And so I registered in December 1950 and I was back home. To work, to work hard, and to prove that the academic world, IIB or not IIB, had acquired a methodologist of stature.

Which, of course, was the perfect time to fall in love. Head over heels—pierced by Cupid's dart, I could have danced all

night, rotten with clichés and all of them apt—in love. I have
long been convinced that the major religions, for all their
ontological virtuosity and ethical magnificence, have lost out
on the beguiling humour of the Roman Gods. I am even now
quite happy to accept these pagan Supermen and women,
playing their naughty little games with presumptuous mortals,
indulging their capricious whims, and generally messing us
about for the Hell—or Heaven—of it.

Her name was Isobel. She was a Social Science Fresher, and
the most delicate, feminine creature of 19 I had ever met. I was
27, a pre-Raphaelite in love, Degas at the ballet, Gene Kelly
in Paris, Gauguin in Tahiti. Her sweet, sad smile and tiny
hands transported me to realms where I was joyously indifferent
to the grim facts of my Jewish endogamy, and my vow never
to upset my family by marrying a Christian. I drifted, oh,
incurable romantic, from bliss to despair, from happiness to
misery, all turning on the capricious moods of a poppet that
the Roman Gods had thrown into the game because it looked
like settling down into a boring and predictable academic
career.

I couldn't work. I tried. I forced myself to grind away on
Kretch and Crutchfield, and Urwick and Brech, I learned to
read relevant chapters instead of whole books, I produced
essays and papers, and really tried! But oh, how much easier
it was to be drawn into preparations for a new show, the first
musical comedy specially written for LSE, with Maestro Kingsbury coming back to produce and Maestro Wiseman to write
and play the music, and Isobel in the chorus so we could be
together all the time. We decided that this time we would
write about what we knew—the life of a student from Fresher
to Finals. I provided the title and theme song, 'Cap and
Gown', and seven other numbers, and wrote a sketch about a
Marx Brothers lecture, with Val Schur as Harpo, Bernard as
Chico, and myself back behind my favourite mask. Fenella
Fielding was recruited as the local voluptuary, Frank Stygall
was the hapless student, Allan Gershon boomed away every-

where, Al Bermel turned in reams of material and we were back in business. Back to normal. Suddenly nothing had happened since 'Place Pigalle', we were light years away from Finals and IIB and Black Summers and MacArthur being fired in Korea. It was a bigger success than 'Pigalle' and we repeated it the following Friday to enormous applause and laughter, especially when I fell backwards off the stage. There was a huge laugh which suddenly cut off to dead silence as they wondered if I'd killed myself. My head reappeared and the laugh broke out again. Which of course, made it all worth while to me, even if I couldn't move my arm for a fortnight. But I was a very happy fellow and Isobel and I were inseparable, walking hand in hand in Lincoln's Inn, shopping in Gamages, oh, such a happy fellow.

Until the Lent Term. When for some reason, and where women are concerned there is usually none, it all went wrong. I never knew whether what I did was right or wrong, I never knew whether I would be greeted with a warm smile or a wet look. How I needed my mates then, my all-knowing, wise and understanding friends, all so clear on how to handle a woman until it happened to them, how I thanked my stars for Frank and Al and Bernard. Especially Bernard, who would join us in our walks to Lincoln's Inn and make Isobel laugh and leave us happy.

But no thesis was being outlined. Dear Mr Hotopf took me to lunch one day and chatted about maturation—the process of growing up, the acceptance of the fact that our childhood dreams may never be realized, the coming down to earth when we realize what we really are. I think he was trying to tell me something. And my bosom pals were trying to tell me to get on TV and one day we actually auditioned at the NAAFI Club off the Strand and nearly sold the material. And Isobel, in one of her 'on' moods, was trying to tell me I should go into the theatre where I belonged. And I tried to tell myself that I must get down to work . . . and I did. With a supreme effort of will, I hammered out an outline: 'The Psycho-Sociological Aspects of Industrial Morale', and took it in to Professor Ginsberg. To my joy, he was very interested in it, and in his infinite wisdom suggested I call it 'Industrial Morale'. I was back on the beam!

Meanwhile, on the top-most peak of many-ridged Olympus. . . .

'I will not have it, Minerva!' Venus was angry! 'Industrial morale, indeed! How boring!'

'Boring, my beautiful Golden Sister?' said Minerva, polishing Jupiter's breastplate at super speed. 'Boring as the bricks and straw that make a wall?'

'Walls make prisons, and don't you flash your eyes at me!'

'Peace, my Sisters!' Apollo smiled at the Maiden Goddesses. 'He may be building the wrong wall. Let us give the foundations one more really good shake and see if it holds.'

They showered him with kisses. 'O, Phoebus, from your throne of Truth, from your dwelling-place at the heart of the World, you speak to men. What shake did you have in mind?'

Phoebus Apollo played on his golden lyre and outlined his plan, and the laughter of the Gods echoed down from Mount Olympus and Bernard Levin stole Isobel.

Bernard Levin? *My* Bernard? My companion of so many hilarious japes and adventures, my witty, warm and waggish friend, had we not worked in the Post Office that very Xmas to earn some bread, had we not spent the whole time playing chess and let the mail sort out itself? *My* dear old Bernard? Could this be the spineless puppet that she preferred to *me*, Moody, kind, loving, sincere, honest, possessive . . . could *his* be the limp dabs that now besmirched her gossamer fingers on their shifty little walks in Lincoln's Inn, *his* the slack jaw that now sullied the sweetest lips in Christendom when I was safely out of sight?

I decided to kill him. It was the night of the Refectory Ball in June, and the clowns had evolved a slow motion boxing match inspired by, or rather, pinched from Chaplin in *City Lights*. It was a wow, but I felt no joy. Isobel had just told me she was making a clean break for my sake. I cleaned off the

clown make-up in the wash-room with slow deliberation,
walked like Pagliacci down the thirty flights of stairs to the
main entrance and waited there with icy calm to bash his
brains in.

'Do you think you have gone too far, dearest Apollo?'
Minerva was worried. 'Do you wish to destroy the builder as
well as the wall?'

Apollo stopped playing and laughed. 'Mercury, where is
Pan?'

'In the woods, I suppose.'

'Well, tell him he has a little job to do—one of his clowns is
losing his sense of humour.'

Oh, Levin, lustful, lecherous corrupter of Innocence, where
art thou? Come forth from the darkness that I may slay thee
with one mighty swing of my fistbone! For now I shall verily
drive thy buck teeth down thy gab-gifted throat! But wait!
By the Great God Pan, what do I see? I see thee slain! I see
thee lying in the gutter with thy pointed little feet sticking up
in the air. Oh, poor, pitiful creature, oh sad thing I have
done. . . .

I spared him and went back upstairs.

But from that moment I wanted to show them! I wanted to
show them who they had hurt, what a brilliant, talented fellow
they had wronged! I *wanted* to be put on the stage and come
back huge and famous with a big car, and show *her* what she
had missed!

After a summer of pain and emptiness, I came back to LSE
in the Michaelmas Term of 1951, and with Al and Cyril, wrote
a musical called 'Holiday Farm'. I had the grim and petty
satisfaction of seeing the outcast couple watching the extra gay
and lively rehearsal from the darkness of the Old Theatre
balcony; I had the wondrous satisfaction of directing the show
to instant success and a rave notice from Elizabeth Frank in
the *News Chronicle*; and the following term I had the complete
satisfaction of seeing Isobel and Bernard going their ways
separately, their dastardly deed undone, their unlovely liaison

lumbered. And so we became friends again—all of us—not so close, perhaps, not so intimate, but good friends. For nobody could have helped it. The Gods had played their tricks, the tricks had served their purpose, the die was cast, and I was headed for show business.

I worked through the rest of 1952, still turning in papers and consolidating my thesis, but I had become once more the marginal man, on the fringe of two worlds, blurring together like an off-phase projector (I adore a classical finish). For I was now flirting openly with show business, seeing agents, doing a hapless week in Variety at the Granville, Walham Green, a hideous week at the Queen's, Poplar, and somewhere on the way, being rejected, to my great good fortune, by RADA and Clarkson Rose. I managed to keep myself with odd jobs, but it was now painfully clear that I had been at LSE for five years, I was 28 years of age, and I had no prospect of any employment worthy of those long, expensive, illuminating, hysterical, mind-blowing years that I had used up, to what seemed so little effect.

Al Bermel spun the coin. Prolific and assiduous as ever, he wanted to do a revue in the Michaelmas Term. I agreed with considerable reluctance, it seemed so aimless to play any more of these games. But I wrote some sketches and a solo act for myself, called 'Hamlet', in which I demonstrated the way that various comedians would play it if they had the chance. Fenella appeared again and most of the old team, Frank, Cyril, Allan Gershon, 'Fish' Mackrell and Dennis Reynolds, loyal and indispensable as ever. It was called 'Rigor Mortis' and it was another big success. When they wanted to do it for a second night I was quite adamant. No more! But I did. And that was the night that Peter Myers and Ronnie Cass, the masters of intimate revue at the Irving theatre, were brought in by Fenella.

'Moody, do you want to turn professional?' said Ronnie Cass.

A year earlier I would have said 'No!' Now I nodded.

I auditioned for them with Fenella's help at the New Lindsey, a tiny club theatre in Notting Hill. They were enthusiastic but said they were fully cast. So what was I going to do this Xmas? Back to the Post Office, sorting the mail, how about a salesman at Harrods over the season. . . .

Two weeks later, on December 7, 1952, at 11 o'clock in the evening, Peter Myers called me. A member of the cast had fallen out and did I want to join them? On December 31, 1952, *Intimacy at Eight* opened at the Lindsey to unprecedented rave reviews, and I was off on the road to Olympus.

But to this day, I have never actually, officially withdrawn myself from the postgraduate department . . . so you see, my LSE has never, definitely and absolutely, ever really ended.

Jacqueline Wheldon

Jacqueline Wheldon was born in London. She joined the LSE *secretarial staff in 1946. Undergraduate and research student 1948–54. Research, Nuffield Foundation 1954–56. She married Huw Wheldon in 1956, and has three children. Her first novel,* Mrs Bratbe's August Picnic, *was published in 1965. Since then she has been working on a novel, set in the 1950s, in nine books, eight of which are complete.*

(From *Clare Market Review* 1950:
Jackie Clarke
'Said to know everyone in the School, she is one of its brightest ornaments and actresses. A lady who Knows Where She is Going, she is in close touch with all' political developments in all directions. . . . She has numberless pale characters in thrall. . . . What would we do without her?')

*A*t last I spoke briskly. 'What is LSE?' I said. I was Chairman of the local Labour Party League of Youth; they were members, two students, LSE and Oxford. To me Harold Laski meant Labour Party; to them he was Professor Laski of LSE. He was coming to address our meeting. They explained awfully kindly, wonderingly, what LSE was, and it seemed something between a special branch of the Labour Party and a secret society. The Labour Party had come to office in 1945. It was 1946.

A slim, slight man in a conventional grey suit appeared. His dark hair was brushed back, he had a black moustache, thick-lensed spectacles, an old-fashioned air of intense respectability emphasized by an habitual gesture of putting his hand through his buttoned-up jacket and onto his heart. His expression, beadily severe, passed easily through irony to cheerful knowingness. I took the Chair. He at once made a joke; it was an anecdote to do with my having introduced him as 'Professor'. It brought the first wave of amusement in an incoming tide of laughter and applause from this unprecedentedly large audience of over two hundred people. It was a brilliant and enjoyable evening.

What stayed with me from that evening was the revelation that there was a universe of ready learning, indeed a form of existence, the other side of some great abyss that I, personally, would never cross; not from lack of opportunity—there may have been that, it did not cross my mind—but from sheer incapacity. I had never come across anyone who knew so much. Three days later the LSE student said: 'Professor Laski wants to see you at LSE.'

The situation at once seemed as hopeless as it was astonishing. I could not imagine what he could have to say to me; what could I possibly have to say to him? I was nervous and dilatory making the appointment to go to Houghton Street.

There was not much talking for me to do. He said I would go to LSE to work as a secretary. I would then be able to take lectures in my spare time. I would first pass my university entrance examination, and after that I would come back to see him for advice before I started a part-time degree course. He congratulated me on making 'an excellent Charwoman', and he did say 'charwoman' in that unique and unplaceable accent. The Labour Party was not mentioned. The incident, flattering and pleasurable, was entirely unrealistic to me. Six months later, however, Professor R. G. D. Allen, in the Chair of the Statistics Department, needed someone who could type reliable figures and tables. I was—to my amazement and slight discomfort—not forgotten. Tests were passed and the job was mine.

'Settled down happily' would describe best what I did in the Machine Room as secretary to the Statistics Department and in charge of a dozen and a half calculating machines with unpredictable, and in some cases supernatural, habits. Here, day after day, came dedicated machine-users, research students and members of the staff. They worked and I typed. We nodded in passing. They shyly asked my advice about re-calcitrant machines (I got cunning about putting them right) and I shyly answered them. I had a wholly justified awe of the statisticians that was entirely without envy. My mind was on the ideas in my head, my job, and the Labour Party. I was by then assistant secretary to the constituency party.

After some time I noticed that one research student some

fifteen years my senior—there were many ex-servicemen in the school, some doing graduate work—took to sitting every morning at the desk side-on to mine. He looked at me in kindly surprise the morning I told him that I did not read *The Times*. It turned out that I did not read French poetry either, Corneille, Molière, Racine; that Shakespeare had not much engaged my attention; and he took great trouble to put what he thought—having no notion of the actual vacuum itself—these curious gaps in my education right. I read, and at lunchtime we talked about what we were reading. But I did not start the required university entrance course.

With the death of my father I had had a slightly isolated childhood in difficult circumstances. I was always half-deaf and short-sighted and never a great mixer. I liked the company of my familiars. I had unfortunately been asked to leave school at an early age. Somewhere I had developed a 'resistant' state of mind, a barbarous tendency not to want to agree with any generally-accepted opinion from the exhilaration of testing my powers and my vocabulary and giving myself a bit of character. On all the familiar 'questions' I had tackled I had achieved opinions. They were not other people's opinions, I considered. They were mine, and I worked at them, a straw from here, a wisp from there, like a bird at a nest. That was the beauty of them. They made me feel safe. I liked them to be as subtle as possible, surprising, paradoxical. Shy but confident, I was not afraid to speak up with my familiars. I had been content with all that until the night of the Laski meeting. I tell all this because it is important to know that I was an unusually ill-educated person to have arrived at the London School of Economics and Political Science.

What I learned from Professor Allen, who was an extremely forbearing, kind and silent man to work for, was the value of plain English. Think first; write it plainly. I 'followed' what I typed for him while I was typing it, but had no way of recalling it afterwards. That was to turn out to be the case with much I was to read. But at that time I was quite happy serving the department and observing the characters and mannerisms of each member I worked for.

One day, into the Machine Room, *my* Machine Room, a new secretary to another department arrived. Brisk, efficient, this young woman, Betty Bastin, soon explained that she was a member of the Labour Party and had come to work at LSE especially to be close to Professor Laski. She added that she was at that moment doing her university entrance examination. I wonderfully awoke, but without doing anything about it, to this unexpected menace to my self-satisfying status as 'potential student'. It was summer days. One warm lunchtime, in Lincoln's Inn Fields my research-student friend informed me that he had told his wife he proposed to divorce her; after that, he continued, he would be free to marry me. Appalled by this effrontery—for our acquaintance was on a purely lunchtime basis, and then only if the weather was good—but otherwise unmoved and disbelieving into the bargain, I passed on some very penetrating and candid opinions of this state of affairs. It was exactly the kind of thing I was good at—'penetration' and 'candour'. I came in from lunch flushed with success. Betty was bent over her desk reading a book and eating a sandwich. 'Do you know how many people died during the Black Death?' she asked me. I frowned prodigiously. The Black Death? I couldn't place it. 'Half the population,' she said. I did not believe that for a second but I was in no position to argue. It was a crucial, piquant moment. I saw what it meant. We passed our university entrance examination together, except that due to my style of writing and owing nothing to Professor Allen's, I had several brilliant revelatory insights in the middle of the Economic History paper and had to do it again.

It was getting on for two years since I had first been summoned by Professor Laski to LSE. The time had now come to return to him as required. I felt honour-bound; and yet ridiculous and presumptuous to feel honour-bound. Naturally, I needed time for rehearsals. 'You won't remember me, but . . .' I joined the queue outside his door at six in the evening, still rehearsing. My turn. The door opened, the student leaving exchanged a final word. The door closed. I waited. I rehearsed. I turned away, turned back, knocked, went in, shut the door, stood there, 'Ahmm . . .' I said. He was sitting at his desk. He leaned well back in his chair and looked at me over the top of his glasses for several disobliging moments. 'Well, well, well, old lady,' he said. 'It's taken you a long time to get here, hasn't it?' The unrehearsed answer to this inconvenient question was wordless. I blushed with dismay and pleasure. I would, he said, do Government and Economics and come back to see him on a given date after the course started. I was profoundly taken aback.

It becomes ever less possible to believe that an insight into the heritage of our civilization, its art, its literature, its music, its science, its history, can be confined to a few without the grave danger that the many are deprived of the sight of those things which evoke what is most dignified in human nature. To train a man to be a 'skilled agricultural labourer' does not mean that we waste our energies and our substance if we teach him *also* to appreciate the beauties of Shakespeare or Dickens, to recognize why Goya was a greater artist than W. P. Frith, to realize that the music of Bach and Beethoven can bring things into his life more precious than he will find in the music of Sousa or George Gershwin, to explain to him at least in large outline what science is, and how it has developed, and to give him some sense of the movement of world-history, not least of the place of his own country in that movement. None of these things ought to be the private possession of an élite; they are all of them part of the process of making man at home in the universe, of giving him perspective, or helping him to grasp how those forces work which determine his own destiny.·

The idealistic substance of this statement of Professor Laski's, his desire to share 'what is most dignified in human nature', to see an unconfined 'availability' of culture which he did his tireless best to realize in practice, was the reason why I had arrived at LSE. I left, as grateful to him as ever, recognizing the generosity of his feelings, but ready to read the statement with new eyes, critically, and with objection to nearly every one of its assumptions.

One of the things I began to be aware of at LSE was that the sentence 'None of these things ought to be the possession of an élite' is an outcry against the impossible. It is not the case that the élite possess the works, but that the works possess the élite. The 'life' we recognize in great works (that goes off the page working into history) is creative and parasitical and dependent on men as is the life of viruses, which also recreates itself in a host; the spending of vital life in their service is demanded in both cases. The élite as I met it at LSE was at my service; there would have been no 'beauties' of Plato, Rousseau, Hobbes for me to have 'a sight' of, if generations of individuals whom these writers had come to 'possess' had not submitted to serve and to keep these works intact and ever re-creative and re-created. Culture is transmitted through a helpless if joyful service. As the representative of the skilled farm labourer I discovered that we exchange service for service; that as easily and with as much difficulty and as much expenditure of vital life as any other sentient and intelligent person of any other occupational category, I too could become 'possessed', a helpless member of the 'possessing' élite. Alternatively, I could be content with 'a sight', as in economics I was, which did not even become a protective 'shadow of lost knowledge'. 'Availability', I found out, is not everything, and 'possession' not what it may seem.

Now it was work during the day, lectures in the evening; and the Labour Party on the side. In the Machine Room I was typing the documents that became the first Cost of Living Index. I typed R. G. D. Allen's *Statistics for Economists*, the first book I ever saw in the writing. I had become acquainted with the beauty of the supply and demand curves in a perfect market, I had learned the best place from which to hear and see lectures. I very much enjoyed, as I always had, writing essays. I got my first 'A' for an economic history essay. As if this was not contentment enough, my tutor suggested I should expand it to put in for a State Scholarship for Mature Students. I was flattered and delighted; but I suspected misplaced confidence. I was quite content to have the essay as it was. I had no eye on a state scholarship and full-time study—I was a fantasist but not quite so unrealistic—until Betty let it be known that she was writing an essay: to put in for a state scholarship. It was instantly clear to me that *The Social and Economic Consequences of the Rise in Prices in the 16th Century* had to be expanded. The run of the library was sheer pleasure. Poetry was not missing, verse was included. There was the wholly agreeable task of making my own impeccable tables of statistics; footnoting. By the end I even knew something vaguely about the Tudors. The essay went in and I got a state scholarship to be taken up when I was 24. Betty did not get a state scholarship; she got a Leverhulme of much higher value, became a full-time student immediately, and went on to become President of the Union. Here our ways, so profitable to me, parted.

Now and again, as a full-time student, I saw Professor Laski in his room where in the early evening he more often than not kept open house for students of all levels. One simply joined the queue. He would read my essay, set another, and afterwards there would always be a new story. I remember, on one occasion, the question was the relationship between ministers and their permanent civil servants. He had a manner of punctuating his sentences that produced unexpected emphases and hiatuses. It went like this:

'In 1927 when Blank was Post-Master General
It is a fact that
After many months
In office
That Minister
Had managed to impress himself
On his civil servants
In one matter only and it was this:
That if a man
And a woman
Were found together
Alone
In a room
On Post Office property
It was not to be assumed
That they had had sexual intercourse.'

Reading his books I personally found them too allusive and
discursive, full of facts and ideas I could not place. I wore a
constant frown. I was a slow reader, naive, turning over words,
ideas and names as I went without much understanding of
what it was I wanted to know from them. Listening to Laski
was quite different, not so much in content—the names unknown to me were still there—as in enjoying the zest of his
own enjoyment. His lectures in the Old Theatre were crowded
as they always had been. He was magnificent at creating
parables out of contemporary politics and those of the recent
past. Had they been the only thing he had to offer he could not
have been so influential a teacher. The most important thing
about him was that he was a generous man of lively temper
who desired, even when it was impossible to perform what he
desired, 'to confirm the lowliest in the possibility of what they
might become' as much as he relished the company of the
great and powerful. This generosity informed his attitude to
political institutions. They amused him, fascinated him, dis-
pleased him, entertained him, he respected them and knew

them; and whatever his theory about them—he was enthusiastic for reform and the 'march of intellect'—what was passed on to me was his enthusiasm for the study of political institutions, a hearty respect for the American Constitution and a respect and affection something near patriotism for the British Constitution.

At the end of my first year, in one of the last conversations I had with Laski, he told me that at all costs I had to stop what I was doing and start again on the B.Sc. (New Regulations). It was, he said, a very superior degree course, with a whole year on your special subject at the end. Back I went once more to the beginning.

When he died in 1950 on March 24, the School lost a great character, and a great teacher; some of his Asian and American students lost a substitute parent. His slight, neat figure, walking uprightly about the corridors, often in conversation with someone renowned, had visibly represented to us the way in which LSE was at that time joined to the world of practical politics and had a vicarious relationship with the great of that world—American Presidents, judges, senators, Generalissimo Stalin; but also how it was joined in particular to the peacetime reform politics of the Labour Governments of 1945 to 1951. When he died it fell to me to collect for *Clare Market Review* the appreciations of many people who had been his students, friends and colleagues. I remember Krishna Menon, then High Commissioner for India, weeping in his office across the Strand.

There were at the time about two hundred Asians, two hundred Europeans, fewer but still a substantial number of Africans among us at the School. We mingled, and our talk, our aims, our problems as they concerned our work, were of the same kind. Our customs and manners were allowed for, not without some misunderstandings. An African acquaintance of mine on one occasion gave a polite reception and during it

invited me into the next room to show me a collection of
Ethiopian paintings; and there we had such a misunderstand-
ing. 'Why,' I demanded, highpitched and ruffled, 'when I
first resisted'—and I had triumphantly resisted—'did you not
stop?' He squared his shoulders in dignified fashion. He
apologized, polite, manly, hurt and puzzled. 'I understood
that it was the custom in England for women to resist,' he
said. Afterwards he sent me a copy of Donne's poems inscribed:
One of the few of my acquaintances who is both English and a man. It
might easily have been the occasion for hostilities to break out
on another flank.

Whatever our native origins, we shared fables. It was
said, with bated breath, that Professor Robbins had once,
before the war, been chased through the Refectory at
lunchtime by an enraged student armed with a knife. The
appalling thing was to imagine how any student could be so
very bold and out of his senses to even dream in the smallest
way of molesting the Professor Robbins we looked upon with
awe. More baffling was trying to imagine anyone at lunchtime
being able to chase through the Refectory, as we knew it,
where 1200 lunches were served in a space where only about
200 students could sit down at any one time. The friend who
remarked, irritated, a few years ago: 'You LSE people, you
always set yourselves apart and talk as if you were some
special incestuous race,' clearly had no idea from her own
education at Oxford of the remarkable physical proximity
we enjoyed, how 'the heat is increased by the contiguity of
many grains lying upon one another', how we constituted 'a
continuous mass, whereof all the parts are in uninterrupted
contact'. It never occurred to me to enlighten her. 'True,'
I agreed smugly. 'Inexplicable.'

If the immediate physical confines were limited, we had
London on our doorstep. LSE pulsed with the pulse of the
capital, with the House of Commons and the politics of the
day. Richard Crossman, Ian Mikardo and many of their
Labour and Conservative colleagues were not infrequent

visitors; the *New Statesman* office was just round the corner and Kingsley Martin another visitor; Krishna Menon, an ex-student, was in and out. We had the pick of visitors to London, film-makers, writers, lecturers, politicians from overseas. Whatever happened in Whitehall and Westminster happened only a walk away and in a short time was being reported on the presses of Fleet Street; we were in Fleet Street for all practical purposes. 'The Lord High Chancellor in his High Court of Chancery' kept us company at Temple Bar on foggy days; Lincoln's Inn, Mr Tangle and all was next door. Dickens's London was all round us. There were walks, after the offices closed, into the empty City of London with all its fine, bombed churches, the fascination of the bombsites, those arcane worlds of wonder. We had second-hand bookshops, where bombed and mouldering books serving every interest known to man could be had; we had London Transport's Lost Property Sales shop which Dickens would have loved, the foreign service of the BBC at Bush House where foreign students had foreign friends; we had the pubs in the Strand and Fleet Street, the Thames and its bridges, the theatres—the Old Vic at hand, Covent Garden, the Watergate hidden away underground at Charing Cross, where the little theatre provided piquant reviews featuring King Farouk and the restaurant crunchy ham sandwiches and the new sort of salads, and good coffee that drew us when we were in funds. There were the concerts and the art galleries, Johnson's House, Sir John Soane's extra-ordinary and endearing museum, the British Museum. If LSE seemed sometimes like a hive of 'pure and exalted activity' it is hardly surprising; it was indeed in the heart of 'the spoken world'. I enjoyed it very much between eight and nine o'clock at night when it had emptied of nearly everyone but the older, quieter, differently-motivated evening students, a few young late-workers. Then the bones of its history and purpose seemed to shine out in its dusty, littery, unexalted corridors and almost deserted library. It was a time to be grateful and pleased not in a spoken way.

MY LSE

Much of what I was studying had an uncomfortable vagueness about it. 'Economics is what economists do,' one notable book had quoted promisingly as a beginning. But it thereafter, for me, declined into what it itself called 'the hopeless confusion of unrelated principles'. In political thought there were words and phrases in the commentators that worried me. *Nature, Will, Natural Law, Social Contract.* There was no having them obedient, straight and steady. Two questions, vague ones, I kept asking myself on 'off-days'. 'Where, oh where is there a beginning?' and 'What exactly am I supposed to be *doing*?' If I distrusted the subjects, I distrusted myself even more. I had no history, no mathematics, no science. I was well aware of it.

Paradoxically, I was 'keeping up'. Fortunately, the average student in good health is a resilient and optimistic creature and the life of being bumped and dragged along like an old tin can tied to the tail of a galloping horse, with the sense it gives of at least going somewhere, albeit in a dishevelled condition, destination unknown, is not permanently, or even for long, disabling. Delight will have its way.

I was particularly fortunate to have for supervisor for a year Mr Morris Jones. He was quiet, merry, not to be rushed; he had a decent respect for apathy. He had, as I remember, a most mild and reasonable manner of asking totally confounding questions and waiting in patience and silence for an answer. Salutary.

Mr William Pickles: now there were lectures—on French history and politics—with meat to get your teeth into. And Professor Smellie was always a great pleasure to listen to, especially if you could get him—it wasn't too difficult—to talk about Shakespeare. Then there were Professor Popper's forceful lectures: no sense of vagueness here in this self-contained world of the Logic and Scientific Method course where I had my first memorable and lasting lessons in the procedures of science, the work of the testable hypothesis; the difference between 'knowledge *how*' and 'knowledge *that*'. Critical notions, which became lamentably debased in the wear and tear of student disputation, flowed from his lectures into the rest of our work. In the gloom of Smoky Joe's as the little café next door was then called, we sometimes had revelations but more often than not added dark to dimness.

To take Professor Laski's Chair in the Government Department Professor Michael Oakeshott came from Cambridge. He was unknown to the LSE students I knew. He wore a honey-coloured velvet jacket and a red tie. He had a secretive, attractive, fine-boned face (and still has I am happy to say), an inquisitive, mischievous expression all in the eyes, a falling lock of straight hair, and a delighting smile; but an inward-turned man he seemed. (A year or so later a headmistress being entertained at an LSE reception told a member of the Senior Common Room that she would never send her girls to LSE. Why not? 'Your dreadful Professor Laski.' Told that Professor Laski had unfortunately been dead for some time and that Professor Oakeshott, standing just over there, was now head of the Government Department, she scrutinized for a moment the velvet jacket, the colourful tie, the lock of hair, the amused face. 'He?' she said. 'He must be ten times worse.')

Professor Oakeshott was interviewed for *Clare Market Review*. What I remember of this occasion most vividly was setting out a list of his works to be added to this interview.

'You don't want to put that one in,' some editorial person said, picking out *A Guide to the Classics*. 'That's only about horse-racing.'

'*Horse-racing?*' I could not have been more surprised had they said fire-raising. The chasm had been crossed, and I was at the foot of a tremendous mountain at the other side; but awe apparently had not quite disappeared. One had got accustomed to the idea that professors were not arch-angels, that they were human beings who quarrelled with each other and had homes to go to; but writing about horse-racing when

there were all those well-known serious and elevating things
to write about. . . .? I crossed it out.

It was not, of course, 'only' about horse-racing, despite the
fact that it turned out to be subtitled: *How to Pick the Derby
Winner*. But it took time to discover that whatever it might be,
it could not possibly have been a 'guide' to the kind of 'classics'
I had vaguely in mind. Professor Oakeshott turned out to be
quite eye-opening about the function of 'guides' or 'abridge-
ments', such as say 'cookery books', in the business of life. He
duly reinstated *A Guide to the Classics* in the list.

'Rum!' was one verdict; but that was only to begin with.
We had yet to hear his inaugural lecture.

It would be impossible to exaggerate the shock, disbelief,
irritation, in some cases fury, in some cases total incomprehension,
that greeted Michael Oakeshott's words on that occasion.
*'In political activity, then, men sail a boundless and bottomless sea;
there is neither harbour for shelter nor floor for anchorage, neither
starting-place nor appointed destination. The enterprise is to keep
afloat on an even keel; the sea is both friend and enemy; and the
seamanship consists in using the resources of a traditional manner of
behaviour in order to make a friend of every hostile occasion.'*

For most of us it was hard to believe our ears. What had
this *tone* to do with the vulgar tongues and ferments of our
divisive politics? Politics a matter of arrangements? Politics
as keeping a boat afloat on a shoreless sea? Not going anywhere?
It went against the whole ambiance of the place where many
of the lecturers were Government advisers and members of
Parliament were in and out to talk to the political societies; to
say nothing of the School's foundation and history. We were
making history, not creatures of it. The fact that it had
thoroughly upset 'both sides'—right and left—says for it what
it was: the work of a philosopher whose dialectical manner of
thinking was unrecognizable to us.

If rumour was to be believed, the Senior Common Room
was in not much better plight, except there, one heard, there
was argument. There it was recognized that another powerful

philosopher had arrived. There, some detested the lecture and some thought it fine and were delighted and relieved. Among other things, in its last part, it had set out a badly needed account of 'a proper course for the academic study of politics suitable for the university.' It filled a felt need. I doubt if ten minutes later there were a dozen students (if they existed I was not among them), captured by outrage as we were, who could have said what this was. Some of us lived to learn.

That we did so was in part due to the fact that the New Regulations had considerably changed the emphasis of the syllabus. There was now a History of Political Thought from Plato and Aristotle to the Present Day. Here, at last, was something that started at a 'beginning'. Specialized lectures covered the different eras of this overall course. The History of German Political Thought had been added. English Political Thought now began a hundred years earlier at 1715, and in the History Department, European political history had been acknowledged to begin before 1815.

Professor Oakeshott undertook the whole course on the history of political thought from Plato, with all the advantage it is to hear one man's view according to one man's mind. It was, among all else not the least, an aesthetic pleasure to listen to these lectures which combined rigour and economy with felicities of vocabulary and syntax that gave delight and insights; and all this brought the whole self of the listener to the lecture and not just the will and the notebook.

Having glimpsed a 'beginning' and wonderfully bold now, I went headlong into it. The first book I really read in my life, ignoring all introductions, prefaces, commentaries, was Cornford's translation of *The Republic, or Concerning Righteousness*. 'We are discussing no trivial matter, but how a man should live . . .' I abandoned my intention to specialize in economics.

Soon I was reading and endlessly discussing dazzling essays by Michael Oakeshott in the *Cambridge Journal*; but it was not until after Finals when I began a thesis (unfinished) on Comparative Method that I read his really difficult book,

Experience and its Modes, written in 1933. Like all great works, the book creates a world to be returned to again and again with profit. The invitation is always to join in an exploration, in the enterprise of realizing, experiencing the world it makes available. Taken with the essays what is offered is a *mind at work*; thought 'creating and engendering itself'. In copious images and illustrations, nothing under the sun of this world we live in is alien to it, not friendship, nor poetry, nor farming, nor fishing, nor cookery, nor religion, nor science, nor politics, nor history, nor the rationalist, nor the conservative, nor language itself, but everything is transformed in its light. A gift of world without end, it is a very possessive one. It possessed me.

After about five months of slow reading I finished it, it says in the last note I made in it, at 1.35 pm on Friday, February 20, 1953. Attaching such a date to a book had never occurred to me before, and has not since. But it was inspired by the same kind of elation, I imagine, as an astronomer has when he has made a new sighting.

What with Harold Laski to guide a way in and Michael Oakeshott to point a way out, to say nothing of the tributaries explored on the journey, LSE had changed my life. I returned to this daily world with the gift of more of my own mind than I knew I'd got. What more can be asked of an education? I departed resolutely with my gains.

B.K. Nehru

Aubrey Jones

Norman MacKenzie

J.W.N. Watkins

Robert McKenzie

(Gemma Levine)

Lady Jacqueline Wheldon with her
husband, Sir Huw

Ron Moody (right) with Al Bermel (left) and Cyril Wiseman

Bernard Crick

Kenneth Minogue   *Colin Crouch*

Chaim Bermant

(Gemma Levi

The teacher lives on . . . Illustration by Ron Moody from the Clare Market Review
Laski Memorial Issue, Michaelmas 1950.

Bernard Crick

Bernard Crick studied at University College London as an under-graduate but went to LSE in 1949 when he changed from Economics to Government in his third year. Two postgraduate years at LSE followed with first Kingsley Smellie and then Michael Oakeshott as tutor. He was a postgraduate student and then Teaching Fellow at Harvard, Assistant Professor at McGill University, 1953–54, and held a Rockefeller Fellowship at Berkeley 1955–56, completing his Ph.D. and first book, The American Science of Politics. *From 1957 to 1965 he was on the staff at LSE, writing* In Defence of Politics *and* The Reform of Parliament *in this period. From 1965–71 he was Professor of Politics at Sheffield University and since then has been Professor and head of the joint postgraduate department of Politics and Sociology at Birkbeck College. He is joint editor of* The Political Quarterly *and writes and broadcasts widely on politics, literature and theatre.*

My LSE was a year or more as an inter-collegiate under-graduate student. then two years as a post-graduate student (1950–52), and then from January 1957 to June 1965 as a member of the staff. But I am only going to write about what I can *now* remember about what it *seemed* to me to be like then as a student.

So this has no pretensions to be either history or premature autobiography. True, I've dipped into some old files labelled 'Student Junk' to get some colour, but they are almost as incomplete and as idiosyncratic as memory; and from my work on Orwell's biography I've discovered that human memory even over twenty years is unreliable, patchy, rationalizing and imaginative unless checked point by point with the written record.

The great tradition of LSE as the Sacred College of Social Democracy, the advance guard—if not the whole army—of the social sciences in Great Britain, and of 'the empire on which the concrete never set' (whose joke was that really?), all that I saw later but not then. How accidental it is that any individual goes to any particular place and, I scorn teleology, to feel part of an academic tradition is always hindsight. True, I was never more pleased than when *The Guardian* made me part of that tradition. The back cover of the Pelican edition of my *In Defence of Politics* has their reviewer saying:

'One of the most thoughtful products of the political dialogues of the London School of Economics since the great days of Tawney, Dalton, Wallas and Hobhouse.'

Youthful ambition fulfilled? No, in fact, socialist though I was as a sixth former, I neither knew of LSE in these terms nor wished 'above all else to go there'. It was accident. I was simply a late developer, nothing but a formidable rugby player, until I prematurely ceased to grow and did unexpectedly well at the old Matric in the Fifth Form and even better in Higher Schools, except that I stubbornly refused to pass Latin even at the lower level. What, at such a school at Whitgift, could be done with me? A socialist sixth-form master spotted that the Economics Faculty at London required no Latin. So he coached me for the now long-abandoned London General Entrance Examination. Almost all of what he taught me, somehow I unloaded on to the paper.

My first contact was, however, a false dawn. I was interviewed by both LSE and by University College for scholarships. My memory of the LSE interview is cloudy, except that there were too many people there, at least six. They took scholarships seriously then, so outnumbered, outgunned and overawed, my stammer kept locking me up as they bombarded me with difficult and even trick questions (of a kind that they had probably had in Army Officer Selection Tests), showing off to each other furiously. No, I do remember one question and I still blush. 'Why do you want to study Economics particularly?' I should have said: 'Because I have no Latin and didn't realize until now that there are other options in the B.Sc. (Econ.)' But I had already rationalized my history, so I said: 'Because the post-war world in many vital respects needs changing, particularly as regards the sharing of incomes more equally.' I still remember the savage, almost tipsy, academic laughter of those brutes. The interview at UC was much more calm and gentle: an immediate offer of a place to do History, as long as I caught up my Latin by the end of the first year.

But the Latin frightened me off and the unknown God of Economics called me on. A formal offer, despite the interview, came from LSE first. But I hung on a few days in hope and fear, and an offer came from UC to enter their small but excellent Economics Department.

Within two years I had so rationalized my decision that when fellow activists in the young NALSO would ask why I had gone to UC for Economics rather than LSE, I'd reply (with an ignorant knowingness): 'It's a smaller department; you see more of the staff; LSE is too impersonal; the staff are all wrapped up in research or public service or making money in the city.' But the real truth slipped out years later when Sir Alexander Carr-Saunders conducted his last appointment's committee for an unexpectedly vacant post in the Government Department. The only candidate put forward was me. It should have been a very relaxed occasion. But not for Carr-Saunders. He cross-examined me like a QC trying to discredit a hostile witness in a murder trial. Suddenly he said: 'I see from your file that we offered you a Leverhulme scholarship ten years ago and you turned us down in favour of UC. Why?' Isn't it said that in interrogation sometimes the sudden, disconnected, unexpected question based on a small, intimate truth will break down even an experienced double-agent? 'I didn't know the least thing about it at the time,' I blurted out. 'This place looked to me just like my father's insurance office. The portico at UC looked what I expected a university to look like.' To everyone's surprise Carr-Saunders thumped the table and said to the others: 'He's quite right. Just what I'm always telling you all this place is like and that's what we're up against.'

The point I'm trying to make is that part of the excellence of LSE is that it is part of London University and that inter-collegiate arrangements can work. It is at its worst when it forgets that. This is not hindsight. I have felt this as man and as boy and was persistently irritating in saying so while on the staff at LSE.

In fact, although I enjoyed UC greatly for the variety of

students there, I was at odds with my subject. My tutor, Alfred Stonier, a brilliant man, in the first week of the first term of my third year, gave me back a vacation essay on 'Value Theory' marked Alpha Plus, but said: 'Get out. I advise you to get out. You plainly don't believe in the subject. You will be a brilliant critic of it if you go on. But you don't believe that economic theory is anything else but an analytical card-castle. If you go on, you'll end up by hating your subject, hating yourself, and feeling you've wasted your life.' Both our pipes went out and I gaped at him. The vehemence of the advice and, in every sense, its personal nature, was obvious. I rallied and relit with a kind of sarcastic meekness: 'I see what you mean, but I am taking finals this summer. A bit late to switch?' 'Nonsense, not if you really want to get out of Economics. You're going along to LSE for Laski's lectures for subsidiary. Government's easy, just reading books. Switch to that till you're clear what to do.' I said: 'Will you give me till tomorrow morning to make up my mind?' 'Of course. Come back tomorrow. I'll make time for you.' I only consulted with my girl-friend in the Philosophy Department. She had already reached the same conclusion about me; and Freddie Ayer and his circle had already reached the same conclusion about Economics—that it just didn't live up to the verification principle.

So I heard Laski's lectures for two years. I got to know him a little, since I was welcomed as a kind of sinner who had repented when I told the tale of my 'conversion'. Doing Government at LSE then was to sit at the feet of Laski. His lectures had a Gibbonean rhetoric about them and he sounded like a Churchill of the Left. No wonder, when chairman of the Labour Party in 1945, he had tried to take on the great man himself; and that the great man had condescended to notice him, trading blows and insults. He was in the Pantheon, of course, of Sagittarius, whose satiric verses we read weekly in the *New Statesman*. Vicky drew him in cartoons as we saw him when he lectured: all head, only a frail and irrelevant body, and standing absolutely still. He poured out his alternately majestic and sarcastic periods without notes, to crowded and often excited audiences, seemingly as if it was General Will himself (who had been to Oxford and Harvard) speaking to us directly. By 1949–50, however, he looked tired and ill. The jokes and quips were always the same. In lecturing on the political thought of the French Wars of Religion one waited, not in vain, for the famous quip to follow the famous quotation: 'the wars lasted until Henri of Navarre decided that ''Paris was worth a Mass''—which indeed, I can personally assure you, it is'. But that year I heard him give the same lecture twice. We did not interrupt him. The mood was anxiety and sympathy. His tiredness was obvious. A few nights later he spoke at the Conway Hall in support of Santo Jeger (Lena's husband) in the General Election Campaign. His name filled and flooded the hall. I was organizing the over-flow meeting in Red Lion Square outside, having knocked off from preparing for Finals to be Assistant Agent for Holborn and St Pancras for a month. Laski was very late. I remember the anxious expression on the face of Norman MacKenzie, who seemed to be in charge of getting him from one meeting to another. A job to get him through the crowd; but to give a rather tired replay of old passages, good for the students, perhaps, but what would the constituency make of: 'It can be said of the leaders of the Tory party, as Bagehot said of the House of Lords, ''the cure for admiring them was to go and see them'' '? Who was Bagehot? And were they that repulsive to look upon and where could one see them?

Yet he moved one deeply. He was concerned with the condition of England, the future of the world, and was both an egalitarian and a libertarian. It was not a matter of philosophy or logic that the academic subject should be relevant to political practice, it was a matter of basic belief; and that I've never wanted to shake off—though the relationships of theory to practice are more varied than Laski would ever admit. He mocked Hobhouse's version of the 'General Will'—'one is unlikely to meet it walking down Houghton Street'—but he invoked, promiscuously and imprecisely, something called 'the felt needs of our time'. He was a great influence on many who went to LSE and others far beyond. His greatness was as a teacher and preacher, not as a political philosopher. Herbert Dean of Columbia University wrote a solemn book about the political thought of Harold Laski which simply applied the dreadful Oxford textual critique, the witch-hunt for contradictions and inconsistencies with which Laski's writings were riddled. He missed the point. The same thing had been done to Rousseau, but the man remains. Laski was wise on Rousseau: 'Do not falter at the formal contradictions of his arguments, which are legion, but endeavour to discover what is the animating inwardness of the man.' Kingsley Martin's biographical memoir of Laski should have caught his inwardness, but it was a hasty and (some say) a largely ghost-written book (and the poor ghost might have done better on his own). We thought at the time that Ralph Miliband was the truest and strongest of the disciples. Perhaps he will write about Laski one day. Or perhaps Ralph, from his very different Marxist perspective, felt, as I did, a certain intellectual embarrassment at reading the books again, some of them anyway, shortly after Laski's death, after the voice that carried conviction was silent. All but the early ones are so repetitive and rhetorical.

Another great teacher dominated my undergraduate LSE —Lionel Robbins. What a contrast! No rhetoric, but well-ordered notes and a slow, logically constructed and ponderously delivered argument. He took his time. For although his introductory Economics course began in October, he would not, so thoroughly was each basic assumption of classical economics argued, even allow Man Friday to join Robinson Crusoe on that hypothetical island for an exchange economy to begin until nearly Christmas. Some were bored and appalled. But most did see what the game was about. He realized that it was absolutely necessary to convince people that Economics is about price, not about the creation of wealth. The Marxists,

even then, called this ideological. But I accepted it as part of
the human condition and still do. Everything purchased,
everything gained, is at the cost of something else. Demand will
always exceed supply, particularly in relatively free societies.
I would, of course, moralize and politicize all this. The price for
political progress may be worth paying, but we had best not
deny that it is paid, especially if paid by others. Then, as now,
I saw these basic propositions as being equally applicable to
socialist and capitalist economies. Also Robbins's basic method
made a great impression. Did he say in so many words—he
certainly implied it—that the great mistakes and choices are
made at the very beginning of thinking about basic concepts
in the social sciences, not on the postgraduate or high scholarly
levels of elaborating and quantifying theories? Any educated
fool can elaborate but it takes a very special kind of wise
simplicity to establish the elements of a subject.

That there was a coolness between Laski and Robbins somehow percolated downstairs, even in those remote days of
discretion. It was thought to be personal and political, but at
the time I saw it as primarily intellectual, seeing only what
showed. And I see no need to revise that judgement. Laski's
crowd rarely went on, for instance, to Popper's seminars. But
Robbins was plainly reading Popper closely (though the clash
of personalities may have been just as great for all I knew), and
something of this came over. Yet Laski and Robbins had in
common two very important things for LSE. They each taught
the basic first-year course in their subjects and they taught it
at a time (five or six o'clock, I forget) when the evening students
could attend as well. So we all heard the two great men and
they saw the importance of impressing their views of the subject
directly on the undergraduates. It gave an intellectual coherence
to the whole school. My private theory of the peculiarly local
conditions for the *troubles* at LSE of 1966 (and after) was the
neglect of undergraduate teaching when Robbins gave up his
lectures, some time in the late 1950s, and went off to become
Lord High Everythingelse. 'Neglect' is perhaps the wrong

word, for when he gave up these lectures, whole committees gave thought to how best to develop them; and the best of the young economists went in as a team to introduce the new models and mathematical theorems of the discipline to the ranks, having been somewhat impatient of Robbins's literary and philosophical approach which left them 'the real work to do', they grumbled, in the second and third years. But they went right over the heads of most students and forgot to establish those basic propositions that can make the difference between Economics being a humane and politically relevant discipline or a technical tool for the biggest paymaster.

Postgraduate LSE was very different. After Laski's death, there was no centre to anything in the Government Department. My temporary supervisor, Kingsley Smellie, said: 'My lips are sealed, but someone very extraordinary is coming who will bring great changes!' Already there was a sense in the whole of LSÉ that the great political days were over. Indeed they were never as purely socialist as legend has it. In the outside world, the Labour Government had won the 1950 election but was plainly on its last legs. The talk was of 'consolidation', not of any extension of socialist achievements. We socialists summed it up fairly well by realizing that we had just seen five years of reform, irreversible reform, indeed, as I argued fiercely against the 'calamity men' who expected the Tories to put the clock back rather than to accept the new time, but, none the less, it was simply reform. Nothing would ever be as bad again as pre-war, but nothing as good as we had hoped. And the new generation of undergraduates had mostly done their two years' military service (I eventually dodged out by pretending to be barmy), were that much older, but had not been through the war like those who had come up in 1946 and 1947.

In my own case, LSE meant less to me than others and its student politics seemed to me less interesting than the UC Debating Society, of which I actually became President after leaving the College. At UC also I had been in on the founding of

a Labour Club to rival, very successfully, the Socialist Society
(affiliated to the communist-dominated Student Labour Federation), and as chairman of the London Association of Labour
Students, I was wise enough to see that the LSE Labour Club
was a kingdom to itself. The London Association did waste one
meeting on LSE (bringing coals to Newcastle) with Nye Bevan
as speaker. Actually, he disappointed the huge audience. He
tried to be academic for the occasion, repeating most of
Laski's favourite quotes from the Putney Debates, 'The poorest
he that is in England has a life to live as the greatest he', etc.,
which I later discovered mostly came from a little book by
H. N. Brailsford. But afterwards at the urinals, he really did
say to me—for he was a sensitive and empathetic man, and
plainly I had had a regressive effect on him when I had introduced and thanked him: 'Lad, I con-g-g-g-g-g-ratulate you.
You've g-g-g-reat c-c-c-courage. I had to c-c-cure myself of
stammering when a young man by t-t-t-aking up p-p-public
speaking.' I loved him from that day, never met him again, but
went to his Memorial Meeting years afterwards on the tops
above Dowlais and wept.

Perhaps also the University Scholarship of £275 a year,
twenty-five more than the maximum Ministry undergraduate
award, kept me out of LSE a good deal, being able to afford,
with that extra ten bob a week and beer at about ninepence a
pint, something of that life of 'sub-Bloomsbury', the pubs
where there was always someone one half-knew, talking
politics or literature, in Frith Street, Rathbone Place, Charlotte,
Marchmont, Lambs Conduit or Great Russell Streets. LSE
types rarely got up into Bloomsbury or even the Museum area.
They stuck close to home in the White Horse, the George IV,
and their own very good Union bar, The Three Tuns, which
used to be on the corner of Houghton Street and the alley
way to the Law Courts, and was always well used by the more
matey sort of staff.

And yet, if I had no sense of an intellectual centre to the
School and if my interim supervisor, Kingsley Smellie, showed

little interest in my thesis topic, 'The Method and Scope of Political Science: the problem of the integration of empirical social research into the study of politics', yet, on reflection, I did nevertheless sample a lot of other things. I went to Popper's seminar. I had been to his brilliant undergraduate lectures on Method, but only the inner circle were allowed to take part in the seminar, except for a specially invited 'victim of the week'. His function was to explicate in a long paper, of which he could get out but a few paragraphs before the dogs attacked him, some fallacy like Psychologism, Historicism, Holism, Determinism, Marxism, or Essentialism, which the truly very great man had already refuted. No wonder they called him 'the totalitarian liberal'. The way he conducted a seminar was intolerable. One felt a mixture of shame and sorrow for his acolytes; but many of us learned more from his lectures and his writings than from anyone. His influence has been incalculable.

In my trade I am one of those who has always tried to carry institutions and ideas forward together. But recollecting for this essay, why did I, already plainly philosopher and theorist, go voluntarily or just for fun to William Robson's seminar on Public Administration, however great his reputation in that field? The dualism must have been there already. Robson's seminars were important, dry and terrifying occasions: he was learned Fabianism personified. We were expected to deliver Webb-like judgements based on Webb-like readings on the whole of post-war planning. Passengers were not spared. William (as I may now call almost my oldest friend) had everything categorized. When I came back from North America without a job, it was Robson who, without power or patronage in that then strangely autocratic department, went through the dutiful gestures of asking me to tea a couple of times, to his house once, even though the power of the keys lay with Oakeshott who in June 1956 had given me my Ph.D., and 'Oh you probably want a job, but there isn't any money in the kitty' all in one breath, then total silence (not a cup of

tea, a sherry or a lunch) until November, when miraculously
'It seems probable that we shall now be allowed to appoint a
new assistant lecturer. . . . It is a quite unforeseen opportunity,
and I shall be most disappointed if you are not available.'
Basically I preferred Oakeshott's bohemian informality and
terse epistolatory practicality, but I came to share Robson's
sense of duty and learned much from him as a colleague and,
finally, as joint editor of his *Political Quarterly*.

To listen to H. L. Beales was my other great optional extra
as a postgraduate at LSE. He wandered, like Dr Who, over all
time and space. But his lectures were of the very stuff of Social
History—whether or not they were called 'Economic History'.
Largely unprepared, immensely erudite and suggestive,
bristling with political implication, many would rank them in
memory alongside Laski, Robbins and Tawney—although for
the published record one has to look not to his own hand but
to over a hundred and twenty (O. M. MacGregor has counted)
dedications or major thanks to him as the prime mover which
have appeared in books or Ph.D. theses by his students. The
chair became vacant one year before his retirement. To LSE's
shame, they held his lack of publications against him. After
the Robbins' Report went off, chairs were filled left, right and
centre on publication lists far less important than his. The
very concentration of talent in one place with very few alternatives, could create much bitterness in LSE—too many people
whose eggs were all in one basket, too many people who had
lived together for far too long. But he continued to teach from
home and some of us still drop in, twenty years later, to cadge
a good idea and a good drink.

As for fellow students, I viewed them rather ironically as a
pretty serious lot. No rags or raids for mascots as at UC. They
stood by while a raiding party from King's removed the Beaver
himself, disdaining to indulge in infantile rowdyism. But you
could sit down at any table in the cafeteria and join in a serious
political discussion or a wrangle about Laski's, Robbins's or
Beales's latest pontification. Undergraduate facetiousness there

was, but it seemed deliberate and pointed to the annual satirical reviews and special occasions, none of the odd, spontaneous happenings that would break out in the other colleges—rags, raids and mock candidates at the Union elections. But at that time I didn't go to these famous cabarets. So I didn't meet Ron Moody and can only hazily remember Bernard Levin, though when pressed by contemporaries over cans of brown memory juice I begin to recall that I was at the famous review when Bernard Levin not merely imitated Laski, but wrote a sketch in which several rival Laski imitators did the great man debating with himself, exposing his own 'stages' or contradictions. Perhaps I was really there but have forgotten. Or perhaps it is all myth. Bernard could phone unto Bernard and ask, but I can't explain all this through a secretary. Anyway, I'm recalling the past, not history.

Yet I have an extract from the Students' Union Publication for 1950 which shows Levin as secretary of the Chess Club, John Stonehouse as chairman and a very rum character called Ken Watkins as treasurer. I can never understand how Stonehouse ever got so far. His nickname at the time was 'Lord John' and his conversation was openly and restlessly about how best to get a parliamentary seat. He seemed to assume that that was the main motive for anyone being active in student Labour politics. He wooed not merely the Cooperative Party, but their Women's Guilds specifically. In the old Coop movement the hand that held the teapot rocked the throne. One afternoon he asked me at short notice to fill in for him at Kentish Town, perhaps trusting the semi-outsider either not to notice or not, until now, to blow the gaff. I began on international affairs and in those days I was a Pacifist, and they were with me to a woman. Elated by this Left-wing surge of motherly approval, I moved on to attack Mr Attlee's inadequacy and Mr Herbert Morrison's reactionary policies. They radiated dislike. Over violently strong cups of tea, they indicated that 'dear Mr Stonehouse' or 'our dear John' would have spoken very differently. He had, indeed, rumbled that the Women's

Cooperative Guild was the one group in the country at that time that was Left-wing in foreign policy (i.e. anti-war: 'we don't want the boys going again') and yet Right-wing loyalists on nearly every domestic issue ('dear Mr Attlee' and 'dear Mr Morrison, not having people getting at them after all they've done for us'). Were they split-minded or were we stereotyped? But, anyway, John Stonehouse rode those two horses together and rode them well. He got his job in the circus.

This essay has become all persons. But that is how LSE seemed to me, not a concept, idea or principle. I only began to think of it in those terms when I was myself a lecturer there (and became disaffected with the reality as a result). So two more people must figure. Before Oakeshott, there was Kingsley Smellie. He tutored me for the year before Oakeshott came in 1951, but I didn't get on at all well with him then, only appreciating his provocative qualities (how well his needling began to move me from positivism) when a colleague. He was a brave man who had gone up to Cambridge on two wooden legs after the first world war. He played table tennis; he kept his socks up with drawing pins; he turned taking the chair at meetings and public lectures from a boring duty into a scene-stealing art form ('It could be said that Isaiah Berlin here, Sir Isaiah, Professor Sir Isaiah, is too well known to need any introduction; but if I said that, you might think it was bluff on both sides, so here goes ...'); and he learnt to drive at about the age of 60.

> *My name it is Smellie I say*
> *I drive to the School every day*
> *Like a tiger on wheels*
> *I delight in the squeals*
> *Of colleagues who get in the way.*

As a colleague I found him brilliant at putting down (or answering truthfully) those direct questions of visiting American Professors which appeared to break the code. 'What do you do,

Professor Smellie?' 'Well, in the morning I listen to a few students read essays to me and then give them a "B + ? —", which is a very safe mark to give; in the afternoon I go to the cinema, there's always something new in London; and in the evening I must wend home to Stephanie and Wimbledon.' He gave a famous briefing to new examiners: 'It's a Fail and it must be a Fail if there's *nothing* on the paper or utter gibberish; if there's something on the paper paraphrasing and embroidering the words of the question, that's a clear Pass; if they try to unpack the question to see what it's after, that's a Lower Second; if they make a shot at answering it with a lot in it you can understand, that's an Upper Second; and if they make a shot at answering it at considerable length with a lot in it you can't understand, that's almost certainly a First.' I've found it in practice almost as good as any other set of Performance Criteria.

When Smellie learned that I was going on to Harvard to finish my Ph.D., he urged me to read Matthew Arnold's *Discourses in America* of 1885, George Santayana's *Philosophical Opinion in America* of 1917, and a funny book by Douglas Woodruff called, if I remember, *Socrates in America*. Oakeshott nodded gravely when I took this remarkable news to him and suggested, in addition, William Faulkner's novel, *Light in August*.

In 1951 I was one of Oakeshott's first students when he came to LSE. Initially, he made little impact upon me. At first he seemed shy and reserved, but then one saw that, unlike Laski, he didn't enjoy argument for its own sake, and didn't care to extend himself towards people who didn't already understand his position or quickly take the trouble to do so. And his position was, after all, a method of understanding, deliberately removed from practice, far more intellectual and academic than Laski's doctrines which could be asserted, simplified and learnt. Unlike most of my contemporaries, I had no sense of shock at his inaugural lecture, only bewilderment. A pity, but why shouldn't there be a conservative political philosopher

(I've always read Burke deeply and admired him much) to follow a socialist? I didn't like their 'but it's not LSE' attitude. I liked Oakeshott's phrase that an academic should not be 'a hedge-priest for some doubtful orthodoxy'. I still thought of LSE as a college of the university that happened to specialize in all these things, not as having a sacred and peculiar mission; and, anyway, I knew that the economists had some right to complain that the public image of LSE ('I'm sure you're not all communists there, are you, Dr Crick?' an old army man said to me) was somewhat exaggerated. But I misread Oakeshott's inaugural on 'Political Education' as being more party political than it was. I didn't at that time understand his philosophical position, so totally different was it from 'mainstream' logical positivist or linguistic schools, yet also sceptical, plainly not 'ethical' (a sceptical Hegelian, was it possible?). Few people understood it. The story Morris Ginsberg's colleagues put around was that they asked him what he thought of the lecture. 'I thought it obscurantist,' he said. But added that he wasn't sure that 'obscurantist' commonly meant exactly what he meant to mean by it, so 'I went to the Oxford Dictionary to check, and it did.' The external examiner in political thought told me that in Laski's day it was all simple parrot Laski, but two years later it was incomprehensible and uncomprehending parrot Oakeshott. 'Which would I prefer?' I only began to understand Oakeshott's philosophical position when I read his *Experience and Its Modes* while at Harvard, fortunately having already been introduced to Collingwood's *Idea of History* by Kingsley Smellie. And when I returned, over four years later, I found a polarized department into which I fitted firmly but uncomfortably.

So 'my LSE' was the undergraduate and postgraduate creative confusion. When appointed to the staff, I was disappointed. The Common Room was too large and impersonal. Beales and Tawney had gone, though I was able to meet them both outside the school. But most departments kept themselves to themselves and generally shop, particularly interdisciplinary shop, seemed (unlike at Harvard and Berkeley) taboo. The librarian did not lack for companions in talking mainly about roses—useful to me at the time. The Government Department had already grown too large, so we were always treading on each other's toes, however many small sections the syllabus was chopped up into and however many options were introduced; and it had partly the air of a court (Oakeshott's new appointments), and partly the heaviness of a good many people who had lost all sense of direction (mainly Laski's old appointees).

Truth to tell, I found LSE a narrow place compared to University College and to Harvard, where the company of colleagues and students in Arts and Sciences relieved the ingrown imperial claustrophobia of many social scientists locked up together. Certainly I earned no love by almost alone, except for Donald Watt, Ernest Gellner, and, I think, John Griffith, opposing the general desire in the School to do our bit and more for expansion when the Robbins Report finally went off and the whole line lurched forward mindlessly. *Beaver* interviewed me, so this is not hindsight:

> We are becoming an ant heap so large that we are losing common themes of conversation . . . LSE ceased to be a scholarly community when the Common Room grew so large that members of the staff did not even know the names of all their colleagues. . . . What London needs is not a larger LSE, but a new college of social sciences. I agree with the economists for once: LSE would benefit from a stiff dose of competition. . . . [And] we should never allow ourselves to become more than half a graduate school; for divorce of research from teaching is as bad as the divorce of teaching from research. It is the first year's lectures that matter—to the scholar as much as the student. . . . The School is now increasingly dominated by peripheral activities of research and vocational pursuits and the hard academic centre seems to be declining.

I would not now argue for another college of the social sciences, like the Yugoslav joke, 'Who wants a two party system? One is bad enough.' I would simply argue that historically the existence and expansion of LSE has held back the development of the full range of the social sciences in the other large colleges in London where they would have influenced and been influenced by other disciplines. We (for once an LSE man, even of my difficult sort, always an LSE man) once needed protection in the social sciences, but we came to need free trade and both local and national competition.

I still interpret the student troubles of 1966 and after largely in terms of the size of LSE, the relative neglect of the undergraduates and *les folies des grandeurs* that result from such a concentration of so many research-minded social scientists all together. And like our poor old country itself, the memory of unique power outlives the reality. Everywhere in Great Britain universities suffer from immobility. But the consequences are worse where subjects are so concentrated. I told a student cabaret, with more public spirit than complete personal honesty, that I was leaving '*pour encourager les autres*'. Yet it was a very tolerant and amusing place to have been in, both as man and boy, and had the overwhelming advantage of being in London, the cultural and political capital, even if its great days both of scholarship and influence were plainly in the past. It is simply that, like the ocean liners, the cinema organs, the cavalry and the Kibbutzim, it has had its finest days. It should not rage against old age but live modestly and remember with pleasure the virile days of its youth beyond recall. My essay has been a middle-aged reflection on what was already, in my youth, a middle-aged institution. '*Odi et amo . . .*', as Catullus remarked.

Kenneth Minogue

Kenneth Minogue was born in Palmerston North, New Zealand in 1930 and went to the London School of Economics in 1952 after having previously taken a B.A. degree at the University of Sydney. For the first two years of his studies at LSE he attended as an evening student. After a year as a lecturer at the University of Exeter, he became an Assistant Lecturer in Political Science at LSE and since 1970 has been Reader in Political Science there. In 1976 he was Visiting Research Fellow at the Australian National University, Canberra. He is a regular contributor to Encounter, The American Scholar, The Times Literary Supplement *and other journals, and is the author of several books, including* The Liberal Mind *(1962)*, Nationalism *(1967), and* The Concept of a University *(1973)*.

E ach year from 1945 on, hordes of young and more or less educated Australians set out on the grand tour. Their base was London, but they made of London an L-shaped village that stretched from Earl's Court to Hampstead pond. They travelled on their thumbs, hitch-hiking their way from the lakes of Sweden to the isles of Greece. Eventually loaded down with Kodachrome slides and a taste for exotic cheeses, they made their way back to embrace the destinies of marriage and a career in Australia. Inevitably a few were shaken loose, staying in Britain to work in universities, or journalism, or (more profitably) to repair the cavities in the teeth of the world's champion consumers of sugar. John Locke had already warned his countrymen in the seventeenth century that too many sweets in childhood would lead to a weakness for wine and women in adult life. He did not know that they would also make the fortunes of a generation of Australian dentists.

I set off on this grand tour at the age of 20 in 1951. In the weeks before I left, I ran across the journalist Murray Sayle late one night in the streets around Kings Cross. He was sceptical of travelling abroad. 'You'll soon be back, old boy,' he said, 'burbling about the fresh greenness of the traffic lights.' But he arrived in London about the same time as I did. This thing was bigger than both of us. My way of getting to London was a job as a cabin boy on a tramp ship, and after a couple of weeks unloading grain in Egypt, and another week in Odessa, loading an UNRRA cargo, I arrived, three months after I had started, in Britain. It is a measure of my foresight and competence at the time that, but for the accident of hitting a British port when I did, I might legally have been shuttled all over the world for another two years.

In this, as in much else, I was lucky. Vast, fascinating London lay before me, and if I did not actually have strands of hay dangling from the side of my mouth, I was certainly pretty green. An Australian education had prepared me at least for the cultural side of things. I knew the tube stations from the Monopoly Board. Every pea-souper (since abolished by Act of Parliament) conjured up Gaslight melodramas and Jack the Ripper. The upper crust came out of Evelyn Waugh novels and my working class was made up of stereotypes of wartime films. Like everyone else, I plugged myself in to the old mates network, and gave myself over to the traditional hobbies of the traveller: lust, and sightseeing.

But eventually an itch for doing something significant invades even the most carefree life. I had no particular reason to rush back to Australia, and I wanted to return with something a little more significant than a rich repertoire of memories. For an intellectual, this meant a degree. Friends of mine were already hard at work at LSE. I applied to do a master's degree, but having nothing more solid to my name than a Pass B.A. (itself but a preliminary stage to what was to have been a Law degree) I was rejected. I enrolled for the B.Sc. (Econ) in the evening, on the grounds that my foundations were distinctly shaky. This is a feeling I now recognize as part of the condition of life—at least I have never managed to shake it off. I was allowed to do the degree in three years instead of the usual evening five. I turned up excitedly for my first lecture in October 1952. It never occurred to me that, a quarter of a century later, destiny would still not have clawed me from the place.

The B.Sc. (Econ) degree to which I devoted my attention was then a masterpiece of balance. Everyone spent the first

two years on hefty doses of economics, politics and history, not
to mention compulsory statistics, before moving on to speciali-
zation in the third year. Even as I arrived, however, statistics
was being jettisoned as a compulsory subject. Much that I
encountered at the School was familiar, but having a personal
tutor was not. At the University of Sydney, in the crowded
days after the war, no such luxury of intensive education had
existed. I was interviewed on my arrival by Ralph Miliband
and assigned to Keith Panter-Brick, with whom I got on very
well. William Robson took us through public administration
and made jokes, such as the one about the man who asked for a
copy of a South American constitution in a bookshop and was
told that it did not stock periodicals. This was, of course, a
time when the treatment of British politics was still heavily
permeated with self-congratulation, amounting virtually to a
theory of British exceptionalism. These days it has the charm
of the antique. Sir Arnold Plant taught us how to optimize
our business resources, in case we had any. If it is economic to
acquire a new piece of machinery for a few hours a week, he
told us, then it is foolish to start expanding operations in order
to use this piece of machinery all through the week. The
lavatories in our houses and the fountain pens in our pockets
are well worth possessing even though we do not make continuous use of them. This I thought very wise. One of the odd
things about writing down what one remembers is the odd
things one does actually remember.

Each evening I would turn up for two or three hours of
lectures and classes, and then some of us would trot off down
the Strand to the Coffee House in Northumberland Avenue.
I had come from a coffee house world in Sydney, but I had
arrived in London just before the vogue for expresso bars. It
was a hard place in which to find a good cup of coffee.

Meanwhile, there was a living to earn, and I was shuttled
all over the Brixton educational division, dealing with everything from charming tots of five to dreadful delinquents of
fourteen-going-on-fifteen. I tried other things. For a time, I

was a Saturday man on *The People*. Earning a few pounds from this source required the utmost furtiveness about any connection with higher education. *The People*'s star man at that time was Tom Webb, one of the heroes of exposure journalism, and the inventor, I believe, of the line: 'I made an excuse and left.' (A later generation amended this to: 'I made an excuse and stayed.') Hermaphrodites were all the rage, and I soon learned that there were said to be thirty-seven medically-guaranteed cases of hermaphroditism in the whole country. Almost my first assignment was to write a piece on one of the thirty-seven, then currently living a dismal life as a woman in a basement room in Moorgate companioned only by a large and alarming dog. The point of the dog, I gathered, was to deal with the derision of the local population. I interviewed this person on a number of depressing occasions and eventually put together the details of her story in the best simulacrum of *The People*'s prose that I could manage. All to no avail. I had arrived at what might be described as the tail of the trend. Since the public was already reeling from a steady diet of hermaphrodites, *The People* judged the story worth about £10. The brother of my subject, a lively and avaricious cockney, turned up to handle negotiations and began with a figure of many thousands of pounds. No accommodation was possible, and hermaphroditism and I faded more or less simultaneously from the world of yellow journalism.

Within the limits of a social science degree, LSE educated me, but it did not excite me vastly. Both points need to be explained. Except where it is evidently technical the study of the social sciences involves strings of assertions for which the evidence is complex, remote and disputable. The undergraduate is required to write essays on subjects where his only recourse is to reproduce what he has read. He becomes, as it were, a ventriloquist through whom speak the 'authorities' of the academic material he has studied, and most ventriloquists are imperfect vehicles of transmission for their masters' voice. There is a kind of built-in dishonesty to many undergraduate degrees. It results from a confusion between the undergraduate and the material he reads, and the only way to avoid it is to develop a special sort of detachment from what one has read. Such a detachment allows one to orchestrate one's sources rather than succumb to the role of ventriloquial dummy. Undergraduates are often advised to 'think for themselves' but this is an expression which incorporates a great deal of cant. The sort of detachment I am describing allows the individuality of the undergraduate to appear in the way he orchestrates his material. This is not at all the same thing as thinking for oneself; nor does it necessarily involve any degree of originality. But it is the essential precondition of both these things, and without it, the undergraduate is in danger of falling into fake enthusiasms and stale ideas. Many ventriloquists graduate successfully, but only those who learn how to orchestrate become fully educated. This is one of the reasons why the study of texts tends to facilitate education. The relations between text, commentator and student are easier to manage than material on the foreign policy of Soviet Russia or the origins of the French revolution.

I was at that time keen to be 'critical' rather than 'constructive' and the social sciences seemed to me to be greatly debilitated by the fact that so many of their practitioners wanted to change the world rather than merely to interpret it. I believed then that to change the world is to become part of it; it is to try and manipulate, and thus to exchange theoretical detachment for practical effectiveness. Academic inquiry required the refusal of such an exchange. It was at this time that I decided to make my fortune (£50 to be exact) by writing a prize essay on some remark Anthony Eden had made to the effect that national sovereignty was an anachronism in the modern world. This was a proposition Eden himself was to demonstrate convincingly a little later in 1956; in the meantime, it was left to theorists like myself. I took a highly critical line about the proposition, and deposited a first draft upon Geoffrey Goodwin who was then lecturing on the Structure of

International Society. I did this in accordance with the common undergraduate delusion that university teachers have all the time in the world, and an insatiable appetite for reading student prose. Goodwin was a model of helpfulness and made a great number of useful comments. I did not, however, win the prize. My essay came back with a comment to the effect that the writer had no sense of 'the vision without which mankind perisheth'. This confirmed my view that the intellectual life was dominated by a kind of flabby, up-beat meliorism.

I was; then, an extremist in the cause of theory, which I counted no vice, and this explains why LSE failed to excite my intellectual passions as an undergraduate. The easiest form of excitement to pick up in youth is some practical commitment of a cosmic kind, usually religious or political. In this respect, I arrived at the School in a condition of cognitive overload. I already knew the truth, at least in broad outline. In addition to Marx and Freud, the bread and butter revelationists of those days, I had been excited by the work of John Anderson who had been professor of philosophy at Sydney. Anderson had absorbed both Marx and Freud, along with the post-Freudians and the latter-day Marxists. What distinguished his work, however, was that this powerful element was combined with an elaborate and sophisticated philosophical position. Anderson was a realist who reduced the complexities of the world to the interaction of complex things in space and time. Theory and practice, geometry and physics, mind and matter and all the rest were subsumed under a unifying formula into a vast complex of happenings, all on the same level of investigability. The knower was just as much a subject of investigation as the known, and was to be investigated in accordance with the same logic. One did not strive to be good, for striving was the character of everything in the world, and goods were perfectly natural occurrences of the theoretical and enterprising spirit. This was a doctrine of great interest and sophistication, but it did have (as it seems in retrospect) a number of spectacular crudities; it certainly convinced the

younger libertarians who adhered to it that they were a saving
remnant living the life of initiative, enterprise and risk in the
midst of a servile, careerist and philistine population. Clear
and tightly drawn battle-lines of culture and the mind were
rather sadly missing in Britain, and it took me some time to
grow accustomed to a cultural world that did not have to be
construed as a battleground. Although I lived an ordinary life
of earning and spending, reading and studying, I was somehow
convinced that the fundamental character of human life was
struggle. I had at the time (I now think) a fundamentally
ideological cast of mind, and I was still under the spell of a
world in which everything that moved was to be understood
as a movement, an abstraction, an -ism.

The dominance of these ideas is one of the reasons why, I
suspect, I did not take fully to the doctrines of Karl Popper
which were then becoming influential at the School. Part of the
reason, of course, was that I was doing many other things than
taking a degree. Another was that I already considered Popper
to be sound on historicism, bad on Plato and dreadful on
Hegel. I then knew nothing whatever of the philosophy of
science and many of Popper's criticisms of traditional British
empiricism and the search for certainty were things I already
held as a result of Anderson's influence. Still, no one who
later had John Watkins or Imre Lakatos for colleagues could
fail to absorb large doses of the vocabulary and mode of thought
which brought Popper to this present eminence. I did go
along to a number of his seminars in later years, and I liked
the precision with which he argued. I had the impression of
one who so loved the world that he could not forbear to put it
right.

LSE then cooled me down rather than heated me up. Paradoxically, the place most open to every wind of practical
political involvement set me off in exactly the opposite direction.
I came to eschew what I regarded as intellectual shortcuts,
but I retained a permanent fascination with the human
propensity to live in terms of doctrines.

Soon after Part I of the exams, I got married and went off with my wife to Ibiza. Each day we padded down a long and dusty path from our house to the town, where we played chess and collected mail. One day in July, I had a letter from the Director to say that I had won the Harold Laski Scholarship. The Mediterranean seemed even bluer for days afterwards. I drank Laski's health in Campari and even forgave him what I regarded as the uncritical meliorism of his political thought. I now had a government scholarship and could work full time for Part II. For family reasons, some having to do with the difficulty of accommodation, my connection with the School in my third year was somewhat intermittent; I knew by this time what I was doing, and I got down to work. The day after the results of finals came out, I went down to Devon to interview for a job at what was then the University College of the South West at Exeter. I taught exactly the same degree as I had just been studying. The following year I returned to the School as an Assistant Lecturer, and this was when my real acquaintance with it began.

The person I saw most of in those early days was Kingsley Smellie, who first appeared to me as a kind of academic Mr Pickwick, cherubic and lively. Coming from a theatrical background, he was accustomed to treat life as a performance, and his conversation swung back and forth between books and contemporary life. In 1915 he was wounded at Ypres, and has since got through life with astonishing sprightliness on two artificial legs. The sprightliness used to be best demonstrated by his skill at table tennis, in the days when that game was a passion among many members of the staff. When he taught, Smellie would point things out with a stabbing forefinger. 'It's all in Rousseau,' he would say, or the Webbs, or Chekhov, conjuring up whole fascinating networks of significance to excite the mind of a student and send him back to the text, reinvigorated to search for that imperfectly specified something. He is by intellectual temperament a Humean sceptic, but he is distinguished by the most thoroughgoing addiction to

progress I have ever encountered. He believes the ordinary
condition of life to have got better with every passing year.
This improvement can be seen in everything from mechanical
gadgets to the steady erosion of sexual repression and guilt,
which Smellie has seen as precisely corresponding with his
lifetime. This sort of optimism does not in the least clash with a
strong sense of cosmic pessimism, partly connected with the
decline of British power in the world. He recounts walking up
Houghton Street just before the war and entertaining three
unlikely suppositions: What if the British Empire should
disappear? What if the Blacks in Africa should prove as trouble-
some as the Indians? What if copulation should be shown on
the screen?

Smellie, like Reg Bassett, Bill Pickles, Richard Greaves and
others, constituted for me a link with the older tradition of the
School. This was in part because, in lecturing on everything
from the history of local government to political theory he
represented a catholicity which modern academic fashions,
combined with changes in the degree structure, have largely
destroyed. It was also in part because he was a repository of
stories about Laski, Ginsberg, Hobhouse and other personalities
of earlier days. Each autumn he and his wife Stephanie
entertained staff and undergraduates from the department in
their house in Wimbledon. A butler of imposing gravity
appeared for the occasion, a huge cat surveyed the guests with
feline disdain, and undergraduates felt themselves part of a
world visibly linked with Edwardian days and earlier.

Among the traditions of the School which Kingsley maintained was that of feuding, and one of his famous feuds was
with his colleague William Robson, a distinguished student of,
and by some accounts, virtual inventor of, the modern study of
public administration. A typical story of Smellie's concerns an
occasion when they found themselves forced into conversation
in the middle of the Common Room. As Smellie told it, they
began enthusing about a recent production of *Antony and
Cleopatra* at the Old Vic.

'Marvellous dramatic technique,' said Smellie.

'Superb,' agreed Robson.

'Such a grasp of the Roman scene,' continued Smellie.

'Quite tremendous,' echoed Robson.

'And great insight into human character.'

'Very penetrating.'

'Even,' said Smellie, 'in dealing with Octavius, a brilliant grasp of the workings of committees and public administration.'

'What?' said Robson. 'The fellow didn't know the first thing about public administration.'

The department I entered was run by Laski's successor Michael Oakeshott. He is in some ways a quintessentially Cambridge figure but has a certain metropolitan raffishness which fitted in well at LSE. He ran the department with efficiency and tact. Lectures and classes had to be given and students supervised, and these tasks were arranged amicably and with a minimum of fuss. Some academic departments are locked in weekly discourse for hours on end. The Government Department met once or twice a year to register any necessary changes, an event whose comparative rarity used to be marked by sherry bequeathed by Rufus Davies who had recently left to take a Chair at Monash. Other meetings were concerned with examinations, and one of the most profoundly educational experiences possible at the School was going over a collection of examination proofs with Bill Pickles giving a running commentary on the proper placing of hyphens, commas, and apostrophes.

Oakeshott was an intellectual personality of a sort I had not previously encountered. To most undergraduates, he was a remote and mysterious figure, and he was often thought to exercise a mysterious influence on Government. A few years before I was appointed, they had been delighted that he had briefly made the headlines of the Sunday press by sunbathing naked on a beach in Dorset, and being shopped by two old ladies from the cliff above. There was about the way he spoke and wrote a world of unseen discriminations whose point was by no means immediately evident.

There are many ways of being a good teacher, but nearly all of them involve the capacity to convey, in one way or another, a world of complexities of which the information being conveyed is but a part, though usually a key part. Academic inquiry is a matter of getting things right, not just right enough, and the commonest way of being academically exact is to use the technicalities of one's subject. But in philosophical subjects, technicalities are largely an inherited lumber, often degenerating into jargon, and may well be a barrier to thought. Oakeshott's cast of mind is to think a whole subject through to its fundamentals, always recognizing that these fundamentals are themselves susceptible to the same examination. I have learned much from Oakeshott over the years, and much of it has to do with different kinds of precision.

Soon after I was appointed, I was invited to see the Director, Sir Alexander Carr-Saunders. I had previously met him once before on the occasion of a dinner he had given for students who had won prizes of one sort or another. On that occasion he had taken us round the paintings in the Senior Common Room, paintings which he had himself collected during the 'thirties. The theft of one of these in the 'sixties was one of the reasons for installing the internal security gates which led to some of the troubles of 1969, and they are now backed by elaborate anti-burglar devices. On the occasion of my seeing him, he welcomed me to the School and extended a memorably limp handshake. I had somehow picked up the notion that the force of a handshake is an index of strength of character, but I also knew that Carr-Saunders had a will of iron.

Experience does tend to massacre cherished beliefs. Soon after I arrived, he was succeeded by Sir Sydney Caine whose background had largely been in the civil service. Caine had the good fortune to preside over the School during the early stages of the expansion of the universities, when money flowed more freely. Augustus is said to have left Rome a city of

marble. Caine left LSE, if not a place of marble, at least the
better for a lick of paint. The SCR acquired a bar, and a
Director's Dining Room which looks a little like a shady
blackjack retreat. In 1967, when Walter Adams had been
announced as his successor, Caine found himself facing the
first of the student revolts imported from abroad—indeed
directed by such imported personnel as David Adelstein from
South Africa and Marshall Bloom from the United States. In
retrospect, this looks merely like a dress rehearsal for the more
serious events of 1968–69, but it stirred life up no end at the
time. Caine remained admirably cool throughout. Indeed, it
was said of him that, having had plenty of colonial experience,
he knew that the natives were ultimately destined to take over
the Government, and that a delaying action was all that could
be expected.

At every moment of excitement, local or national, the
Common Room becomes a place of impassioned discussion.
Early on in my time at the School, Suez and Hungary
dominated attention, and it was as if a wind of division had
blown through English intellectual life. People inclined one
way or another according to their political views, temperament,
current mood; and the way they bent was by no means predictable from their past judgements. Few things are more
fascinating than the obscure happenings in the recesses of the
soul by which people take up positions on public events. It
was at the time of Suez, when I was still working out who was
who in the Common Room, that I saw a large man with
expressive gestures talking volubly to a surrounding group.
This, I thought, with a rapid recollection of the names of staff
in the Calendar, must be Lord Chorley. It was in fact Lionel
Robbins; it was only later that his title caught up with his
personality. In general, the Common Room that I then entered
had little connection with the legendary origins of the School.
In the early phase of its life, the School was a profoundly
British institution, and its academic preoccupations were
closely linked to the impulse of reform. People like Laski and

Morris Ginsberg developed the Fabian ideas of the founders
and worked both to enlighten and improve the world. The
School was closely connected with the Labour Party and with
nationalist movements throughout the Empire. But it had
always been open to international impulses, and especially
from the 'thirties onwards, it was at the centre of the migration
of intellectuals, especially Jewish ones, from central Europe.
By the 'fifties, the sense of mission was a much smaller
element in the make-up of the School, and I would be inclined
to think that its intellectual toughness was considerably greater.
The Government Department was more interested in history
than polemic, and the younger economists had developed a
messianic sense that mathematics was transforming their
subject. The philosophy of science influenced most departments, largely emanating from Karl Popper, and developed by
people like John Watkins and, in time, Imre Lakatos.

Towards the end of 1968, LSE got caught up in another
intellectual bushfire, sparked off this time by the May events
in Paris and the Vietnam War, mixed with local demands for
democratizing the universities. During the late autumn of that
year, frequent meetings were held in the Old Theatre and
something called the crisis of capitalism was discussed with as
much fervour as at any time since 1848. LSE provided a centre
and a platform for politically excited people from all over
London and beyond. In the midst of the turmoil, after the
gates had been torn from their hinges and the School had been
closed and was under police guard, the porters were astonished
to find a little old lady tapping on the doors to inquire whether
they had found her spectacles, left behind at one of 'those
interesting meetings'. Excitement was daily fuelled by a
stream of handsheets. Few people failed to succumb to the
passions of that time, though some were immune. At the very
time the gates were being pulled down, I recall a statistician
emerging from a lecture room (as a horde of purposeful
students went dashing past) saying earnestly to his companions: 'So, if we just change the parameters, then ...' In

the end, the universities proved resilient enough to resist these destructive frenzies, and a large part of its resilience derived from such splendid indifference to anything except academic concerns.

Walter Adams was Director of the School at this time, and he was shaken by what happened. It was certainly difficult not to be. Student militancy has in some moments, usually their beginnings, a considerable charm. I remember a moment when a group of militants sat down in the foyer of the School, tossing cigarettes across to each other and liable at any moment to break into a chorus of 'We shall not be moved'. It was the sort of moment that people experience in revolutions, an exhilarating sense that anonymous routine has been left behind and the stage of history occupied. Most students, furthermore, remained on good terms with individual members of the staff. Oddly enough, staff-student relations are often easier where there is a clear conflict of opinion. Staff who sympathize with the student grievance run the risk of having their supposed unreliability exposed when it is found that they will not follow every turn and twist of what is often a highly volatile set of demands. Nevertheless, student troubles are distinctly nasty events. The sense of aggrieved righteousness that rapidly develops soon leads militants to abuse everyone who disagrees with them. Language deteriorates and the handsheets are full of sneering misinformation. No one who has lived through successions of such events involving separate generations of students can fail to be impressed by the humourless fanaticism and imaginative poverty of those who take part. And there are always a few personalities verging on the pathological who develop an ungovernable hatred of anyone whose loyalty is to the university rather than to the militant movement of the moment. It fell to Walter Adams to endure an extraordinarily vicious example of this kind of thing, and though his policy can be criticized on many counts, he sustained his position with a doggedness that in the end won through. One of the ironies of the situation was that he had profound liberal convictions and he genuinely liked individual students. He had after all organized the escape of academic refugees from Hitler's Germany in the 'thirties. He was certainly marked by what had happened to him, and my impression is that he took a grim pleasure in the sectarian quarrels which reduced the Students' Union to impotence in the years after these events. Nothing that he experienced, however, prevented him from continuing to tell outside bodies that he felt that the troubles the School had had were just a sign of the vitality of the School and its students. This 'boys will be boys' view of the matter seems to me mistakenly to assume that people are only being critical and standing on their own feet when they are shouting slogans in a mob. The life of the mind is Rodin's motionless thinker and the courteous Socrates, not men on balconies or demonstrators in the street; and the one sort of excitement excludes the other. Clarity and cogency of thought are seldom found among militants. They are often to be found, however, in the students who do not make the headlines, and who are implicitly denigrated when the twitchings of militancy are mistaken for independence of mind.

Still, even nightmares have their place in the spiritual life, and the worldwide militancy of the last decade has given rise to a much tougher and more self-conscious sense of what is distinctive about academic life. In many ways, the best place for universities is in quiet backwaters where the distraction of practical commitment interferes less with the pursuit of objectivity. But there are also benefits to be found in an institution placed right at the centre of affairs, an institution whose academic integrity has to be the work not of geographical accident but of deliberate discipline and intent. 'May you live in interesting times' was an old Chinese curse. LSE is in the centre of an interesting place but has managed to make of it a blessing rather than a curse.

Chaim Bermant

Chaim Bermant was born in Lithuania and came to Glasgow at the age of eight. He attended the London School of Economics from 1955 to 1957. Formerly he had been educated at Queens Park School, Glasgow, Glasgow Rabbinical College, and had graduated from Glasgow University. He has worked at various times as kibbutznik, schoolmaster, economist, script-writer (for Scottish TV and Granada), and various newspapers. He has been a full-time writer since 1966 and is the author of eighteen books including Jericho Sleep Alone, Berl Make Tea, Diary of an Old Man, Troubled Eden, Here Endeth the Lesson, Coming Home, The Second Mrs Whitberg, The Squire of Bor Shachor, *etc.*

J hated the place.

I had just come down from Glasgow with a reasonably good degree in economics and politics and the LSE was the natural place for anyone who hoped to continue studies in either, yet I am not sure how it had acquired its legendary reputation. I detested the spirit of its founder, Sidney Webb, through whose work I had had to trudge as an undergraduate —great, flat acres of fact, unrelieved by imagination or insight. There was, of course, Harold Laski, but he had been dead for five or six years by the time I came, yet the place still flowered in my imagination as a confluence of all that was learned, witty and wise, an Oxford without dilettantes. I was, as yet, not quite sure what I would do at the end of my studies, but to have been at the LSE seemed to me an end in itself. Anyone arriving with such ideas, even in paradise, is due for a disappointment and I was no exception.

The first shock was the building itself, a charmless pile, like the head-office of a minor insurance company, hidden away in a back street. Glasgow University, which dated back to the fifteenth century, had been rebuilt in the nineteenth, during the high-noon of mock-Gothic, by Gilbert Scott and it looked like a grey St Pancras, but I liked the mullioned windows, the lofty halls, the towers, the turrets, the pinnacles, the spacious, Oxford-style quads. In the LSE the immediate feeling was one of constriction amounting almost to a sense of imprisonment, especially between lectures, when one could be trampled underfoot by the swirling crowds in the narrow corridors.

The second shock was the non-academic staff. In Glasgow the porters were friendly, courteous and helpful. Here they were none of these things. The LSE goes through (or at least went through) cyclical phases of radicalism and conservatism. In the mid 'fifties it was passing through a comparatively conservative phase, but the porters dated from an earlier age when, presumably, someone took it into his head to emancipate them from serfdom. As a result they lost the cap-touching obsequiousness of the Oxford scout without, however, retaining any of his civility and one encountered a People's Republic style of bloody-minded officiousness. One met it in the halls, the canteen, the library, everywhere.

There was a long-running musical at the Stoll Theatre next door (since demolished), called *Kismet*, whose celebrated refrain (set to Borodin) 'Take my hand, I'm a stranger in paradise', kept running through my mind as I wandered through the endless corridors. The LSE was no paradise, but I felt strange and lost and was a little nervous of approaching a porter for help, for porters were usually deep in conversation with other porters and didn't care to have their tête-à-tête disturbed.

There were many little by-laws and restrictions which were all the more irksome for being pointless. I once wrote a letter on LSE note-paper to the *Manchester Guardian*, and two days later came a reprimand from the director, Sir Alexander Carr-Saunders, pointing out that this was against the rules—and me with the gold braid of my M.A. (Hons) still untarnished on my epaulettes! I felt oddly small and humiliated.

In the Glasgow University library, one had open access to the shelves and one came and went freely. At the LSE access was restricted even for graduate students, and all cases were searched for stolen books. 'We get all types here,' said a porter. 'They'd walk off with a bleeding desk if you'd let 'em.'

There was but one strike during my years at the LSE and that, significantly enough, was over the canteen food which, to my mind, showed a healthy pragmatism not evident in the LSE strikes and sit-ins of a later age. The food was in fact of a quality one might encounter in any college refectory, which is to say, it was not poisonous if taken in modest quantities, but what made it unpalatable was the bullying manner of the canteen staff, and after suffering a meal or two I began bringing sandwiches, a habit which brought me into the LSE Jewish society.

I had in my undergraduate years, and even before, been active in numerous Jewish groups, and had served as chairman of this and secretary of that. When I joined the LSE I hoped for a period of quiet anonymity, a rest from Jews and Jewishness and to that end took rooms in Tunbridge Wells, which was about as far as one could get from both. But sitting in my corner reading the *Manchester Guardian* and munching my sandwiches, I became aware of other sandwich munchers, dainty little creatures with dainty little sandwiches, cut up into neat squares and filled with smoked salmon and cress. They were not refugees from the canteen, but part of the Kosher crowd.

There were so many Jews at the LSE in those days that it was often referred to as the London Shul of Economics. Most of them seemed to be anxious to keep their distance from Jewish life, possibly for the same reasons as I did, but about five dozen or so were members of the Jewish society which met formally about once a week, and informally during the lunchtime sandwich sessions. Most of them were girls and most of the girls read law and I should imagine that there must be a glut of Jewish women barristers by now.

There were also a Zionist society, which was virtually the Jewish society in more earnest mood, and its dominant spirit was a young Israeli graduate student, a lean, skeletal figure, with wide nostrils and cropped hair who urged us to woo students from what were then called 'the under-developed' countries. 'In another five or ten years,' he said, 'these people could be Prime Ministers.' I had in fact become friendly with a Nigerian student, an Ibo, who tried to win me over to the Palestinian cause. I don't think he regarded me as a prospective Prime Minister, but he thought that the Palestinian cause was so self-evidently just that he could not understand how so many Jews, whom he otherwise found to be rational, intelligent and humane, could be Zionists. The Algerian war was then coming to a head and he was convinced that the Zionists would have to get out of Palestine like the French from Algeria, the Italians from Libya and the British from Nigeria. But where will they go? I asked. He looked at me in bewilderment. 'Like all the rest,' he said, *where they came from.* His attitude was, in fact, not untypical. There was much thinking in general terms with little understanding of the special case.

Many of the arguments in the debating societies raged round the subject of colonialism. They were not as one sided as they would be now and were fairly well-informed, but they were a trifle dogmatic, with many, too many, an 'of course', as if the last word on the matter was being uttered, and completely humourless. Any laughter occasioned was usually unintentional. The speakers, and even some of the listeners, took themselves very seriously, as if the future of the world rested on the outcome of the debate.

National Service had just ended so that they were about two years younger than my generation of undergraduates, but they seemed older, with little of the diffidence of youth. In particular they lacked the cheerful conviviality (by which I don't mean drunkenness—though by Glasgow standards they lacked that too) one associates with student life. It is possible that we were immature and they precocious, or it may have had something to do with economics as a discipline, which is enough to wipe the smile off anyone's face, but their earnestness also suggested presumption, a belief that the world was not merely theirs, but was theirs to put right.

The LSE offered but a slight sense of community. One did

not feel oneself to be part of a college in the sense of a *collegium*. As a research student I was something of an outsider, neither part of the faculty, nor of the undergraduate mass, but in my first months at least I was an interested observer of undergraduate life and I felt that they too did not form a cohesive fraternity, but rather a floating mass of individuals working for a similar degree. In Glasgow there were numerous old lags, medical students, divinity students, lawyers, whose courses lasted five, six or seven years, who were there when one came, were still there when one left, and who helped to give the student establishment continuity; whereas in the LSE generation followed generation in rapid succession and there was a constant and somewhat bewildering sensation of fluctuation and change.

The place was full of famous names, Robbins, Titmuss, Oakeshott and others, whose work one had read and admired, but their presence hardly radiated beyond their studies or lecture rooms, and in any case, they, in common with most of the other academic celebrities, were busy men with many lives, serving on this Royal Commission or that public board, and they were rarely to be seen in Houghton Street. Glasgow was not residential (though it had a couple of halls of residence) and the life of the University continued far into the night. The LSE kept office hours. It wasn't quite lights-out at six, but life petered out rapidly thereafter. By seven one could play hop-scotch in the corridors. The LSE was a place of work, a machine, and an efficient one, but not quite a university. There was no confluence of disciplines, no catholicism of interests: it was devoid of the relaxed attitudes one looked for in an academic institution. One felt that if it was put through a wringer not a drop of juice would emerge. It was everything that one might have expected of a school founded by Sidney Webb, a place dedicated to white papers and blue books and statistical abstracts. In Glasgow the economics or politics student read for an M.A. In London one read for a B.Sc. One moved from the humanities to be confronted with hard-core economics. If a man-and-a-half lays a brick-and-a-half in a day-and-a-half, how long before the country goes bankrupt? My own particular interest was politics and in Glasgow the basic texts were Hobbes and Hume. In the LSE they seemed to be McKenzie and Butler. One was forced out of the realm of speculation into the realm of fact and it became clear in retrospect that my antipathy towards Houghton Street had little to do with the LSE and a great deal to do with myself: it was the place where I grew up.

Few of the other research students shared my view of the place, though one Indian student told me—perhaps after a brush with the porters—'I would burn the place down. In here you have everything that is wrong with England.' There was a large contingent of Americans, most of whom looked like budding Galbraiths, long, lanky figures, with short hair, narrow lapels, button-down collars, large ears and huge glasses, who adored the LSE as they adored everything about olde England and they would not suffer me to utter a harsh word even about the building, which they variously described as 'compact', 'intimate' and 'life-size', and they moved about the place with the veneration of pilgrims, to sit, as one of them put it, 'at the feet of the mighty'. It made him sound like a fashionable chiropodist.

Graduates had their own common room with lumpy, coffee-soiled arm-chairs, a few torn magazines scattered about the place, a number of cheap reproductions, including, if I remember rightly, a Picasso with an eye too many, a Van Gogh with an ear too few, some Degas dancers. The appointments of the room I will admit were entirely in keeping with the appearance of most of its habitués. The Americans, however, looked as if they were used to something better, but they did not complain. They may have found it 'life-size'.

We had a dining club whose wine-bill was, on at least one occasion, met by an American, for most of us subsisted on tiny grants which would have seemed substantial in the provinces but which left one on the brink of starvation in London. The sense of constriction I complained of in my opening paragraphs may have been due to sheer poverty; the dining club was something one saved for, like a Christmas club. I suggested that we should have moneyed guests who would help to pay for the meal, but instead we had distinguished guests who generally came with their wives and added to the expense without adding much to the gaiety of the occasion. One exception was Hugh Gaitskell. Another was Lord Attlee. He sat throughout the meal hardly uttering a word, somnolent and frail, like an elderly dormouse, but it soon became clear that he was thinking what to say, for when he rose to speak, with pipe in hand, he was like a different man, and gave a twenty-minute performance which convulsed the audience. 'A funny thing happened on the way to Houghton Street,' he began. It was not in fact all that funny, but coming from that sombre little figure it seemed hilarious.

'Did someone write it for him?' asked an American.

'He's not Bob Hope,' I said.

I had many arguments with the American students, for it seemed to me that their adoration of everything English (including even the LSE) was but a symptom of their disillusionment with America. I had not, as yet, been to America myself, but I had spent the summer reading American history at the Salzburg Seminar in American studies and it seemed to me that no great power in history had used its influence so benignly and with such restraint, a view which brought me into conflict with most of the research students who usually answered my arguments with but one word—bananas! A Leftish administration in Guatemala had lately been 'de-stabilized' through the efforts of the United Fruit Company.

One morning we entertained a visiting party of American Senators and Congressmen who were cross-examined by the American students, among others, as if they were personally responsible for the coup. One elderly, white-haired figure kept referring to 'the Eisenhower philosophy' without leaving one with any certainty as to what, if anything, the philosophy meant. The group as a whole seemed unnecessarily defensive and I intervened with the suggestion that if one must have a corrupt oligarchy among one's neighbours, it was better to have an amenable oligarchy than a hostile one. 'You know,' said my Ibo friend later, 'you're a fascist.'

This was also the time of Suez, and in Houghton Street, graduates and undergraduates, expatriates and natives, were at one in denouncing the Anglo-French intervention, but I felt that Israel, at least, after the continuing loss of life she had suffered from repeated Fedayeen incursions, had good cause for marching into Sinai, but on this occasion even the Israelis turned upon me. It was a novel experience. I was perfectly used to being in a minority—indeed I revelled in it on most issues, though generally when I spoke about Israel even on non-Zionist platforms, I could count on a sympathetic hearing —but now I was greeted with almost personal hostility, especially among coloured students. The concerted anti-Zionism of the so-called Third World, which is today such a familiar fact of life, was beginning to crystallize even then. I began to withdraw from student life entirely and to concentrate on my studies and it was then that I came upon what is, of course, the redeeming feature of the LSE, the quality of its teaching.

I had come to the LSE to write a thesis on the Independent Member of Parliament and I was placed under the supervision of Mr Bassett, a tall, thin, white-haired figure, with a long melancholy face like an emaciated horse. He had written an epoch-making work on democracy and foreign policy, which may have taken him about twenty years to complete, and he was a little taken aback when after about three months under his supervision I turned up with the first chapter of my work, which was about the size of a book. He didn't read it so much as weigh it.

'You're a young man in a hurry, I see,' he said in his slow voice. 'At this rate you'll soon be nipping round the corner for fifty guineas a night', which made it sound as if I was about to become an habitué of an expensive brothel. 'Round the corner' was in fact Associated-Rediffusion (forerunner of Thames Television), which to his mind was infinitely worse, and several LSE teachers, with Robert McKenzie pre-eminent among them, had already established a reputation as TV dons.

Bassett was a don's don whose researches into the paradoxes of democracy had uncovered areas of speculation which had been left untouched before. He expected at least a degree of originality from his students and thus warned me against relying too heavily on printed books, firstly, because they are often inaccurate and by using them I would be perpetuating inaccuracies (which he regarded as even worse than initiating inaccuracies). Secondly, if they were accurate, the information was already there, and to rely on such sources therefore, was not to add to the sum of knowledge, but to redistribute it. 'Are you here,' he asked, looking at me over his glasses, 'to research or redistribute?'

With his help I drew up a list of MPs who had been elected as Independents or had renounced or been deprived of their party whip in the ten Parliaments between 1918 and 1955.

His knowledge of politics and politicians was encyclopaedic and he tended to be somewhat dismissive of both. He also knew a great deal about the private lives of politicians, their habits, their proclivities and listening to him talk, occasionally, was like Aubrey brought up to date. When I mentioned that I hoped to see Sir Harold Nicolson, he said, 'better take a chaperon', a reference to Nicolson's homosexuality which was at that time lost on me.

Of another Member, he said: 'Better go and see him before he drinks himself to death', and he in fact died a few months later, though whether of drink or otherwise I could not tell.

The LSE library remained open till about eight or nine in the evening (though whatever the actual closing time I was flushed out of my corner by the impatient staff about half an hour before that). The building was in darkness by the time I emerged and when I came down the steps into the cheerless dank of Houghton Street, I generally found the lights in Bassett's rooms in the annexe over the way, were still on, and more often than not I would knock on his door to report on my day's findings. I don't know how many students he supervised, or if they were all as demanding as I was, but if they were it is not surprising that he took about twenty years to a book. It is very unlikely that I was always welcome and once or twice I imagined that my knock was answered with an expletive which did not quite go with what one knew of the man, but he would always ask me in, and I would make my way over an obstacle course of books and box files to his desk. I needed the reassurance that I was working on the right track, and these meetings at the end of the day, before the long journey to my bleak rooms, helped to ease my isolation and made me feel, momentarily at least, that I was indeed part of a university. There is a Talmudic precept: 'Let thy house be a meeting place for the wise; sit amidst the dust of their feet and drink the words with thirst.' Bassett was the only wise man to whom I had ready access. There were, I think, occasions when he was glad of my company, and he would sit back in his chair with a cigarette smouldering in the corner of his mouth and address the ceiling in lengthy monologues. When he spoke of a political event, whether the Carlton Club Revolt, or the formation of the National Government, it was as if he was an active participant, but what I particularly enjoyed was his analysis of character rather than events, and his little sketches—etched in vinegar—of Lloyd George, Asquith, Bonar Law, MacDonald and others. I am sorry I didn't keep notes. He was no Johnson, but his knowledge, his insights and his mild acerbity made him worthy of a Boswell. I asked him why he didn't write a political novel and he said—in what I took to be a reference to C. P. Snow—that there were already too many bad novels and bad novelists about.

As I mentioned, I lived in Tunbridge Wells for much of the time I was at the LSE, and coming up on the 7.48 one day, I noticed Bassett at breakfast in the dining car reading *The*

Times and I sat down opposite and greeted him with a cheerful 'hullo'. The hands gripping the paper tightened, and a groan escaped him. It was only then that I realized I was persecuting the poor man and I fled to another carriage.

He was, I think, a bachelor, but I didn't know anything about his private life: to judge by the hours he kept, he had none.

I left the LSE after about two years. I completed my thesis at another university some time later and I wrote to Bassett asking if he would like to see a copy. He didn't reply, which, all things considered, was a forgivable oversight, but it didn't seem like him. It was only later that I learned he was dead.

Colin Crouch

Colin Crouch was born in 1944 and went to LSE in 1965, after having worked for several years as a journalist. He was President of the Students' Union in 1968 and later wrote The Student Revolt *(1970) which includes a detailed narrative of events at LSE 1965–69. He was a research student at Nuffield College, Oxford, 1970–2, and lectured in sociology at the University of Bath 1972–3 before returning to the London School of Economics in 1973. He has been a member of the executive committee of the Fabian Society since 1969 and was its chairman in 1976. Other publications include* Class Conflict and the Industrial Relations Crisis *(1977);* The Resurgence of Class Conflict in Western Europe since 1968 *(editor with A. Pizzorno; 1977), etc. He is currently engaged in research on the political sociology of inflation in Western Europe.*

lthough the late 1960s seem too recent for genuine reminiscence, the extraordinary climate of student life at LSE and many other universities throughout the industrial world in those years now seems so completely vanished that it is already possible to regard it wholly from the outside. Between the year when I first went there as an undergraduate (1965) and that when I temporarily left (1970) the student protest movement had, like a Roman Candle, burst into vivid, fascinating life, sent out its dangerous and irresponsible bursts of flame and sputtered out, leaving an empty shell of rhetoric and redundant organizations to puzzle subsequent student generations to whom the whole affair is but a folk memory.

Since the 'troubles' revived the myth of 'red LSE', and since most of this piece is concerned with political turmoil, it is best to start by setting down a more accurate political characterization of the School as it was then (and is, with some changes, now). With the possible exception of the closed society of Professor Sir Karl Popper's Philosophy Department, all the School's departments could boast a sufficient degree of heterogeneity to render any simple categorization inaccurate. However, the distinct Conservatism exuded by the two largest—Government and Economics—was enough to give the lie to the conventional view of the place, and to perplex those of us arriving as undergraduates with the naive and optimistic assumptions of the early and mid 1960s.

In neither instance was this Conservatism orthodox. From the Government Department came an interesting Hobbesian cynicism mixed with the nervous mistrust of revolution and mass movements that was more typical of European reaction than of English Conservatism. This was determined by the significant number of refugees from various kinds of European totalitarianism who had found sanctuary on the staff of the School, in both Government and other departments. Also, the Crown Prince of LSE Conservatism himself, Professor Michael Oakeshott, could hardly be described as orthodox.

It is difficult to decide whether the devotion of economists to a free-market economy implies a political philosophy or simply a preference for the form of economic arrangements which is most suited to mathematical analysis. Similarly, the irritation which we, as radical students, felt with that discipline mingled political objections with resentment at the technical difficulty of its increasing mathematization. We were also bored by the compulsory first-year economics lectures, after lunch in a stuffy, over-crowded Old Theatre. Even the examples used to illustrate the theoretical points were selected from markets in the dullest commodities—principally, I recall, cabbages.

By the late 1960s our discontent about economics focused on the massive figure of the late Professor Harry Johnson, whose appointment to the School signalled a distinct shift towards the Chicago School of Economics and the deeply conservative doctrines of Milton Friedman which have since replaced liberal Keynesianism as the economic orthodoxy of the western world. Johnson's intellectual powers, mathematical ability, enormous output of work and capacity to commute between a chair here and the one he retained in Chicago, made him a legend while still at LSE. Stories were told of how he had once polished off a major article and a bottle of whisky while waiting for a delayed connecting flight at Toronto airport. He left the school in 1974; his health was weakening and in 1977 he died, aged 53.

The counter to LSE Conservatism were the Departments of
Social Administration with its distinctive Fabianism and Law,
which seemed radical despite the important presence of Professor Harry Wheatcroft who specialized in tax consultancy.
At the centre of the Social Administration Department was the
late Richard Titmuss whose personality reflected the content
of his work and philosophy in the way that one always expects
to be the case but which rarely is. His physical presence and
one aspect of his character were marked by a stern asceticism,
but once that had been penetrated a warm and kind personality
evoked affection as well as respect. Once, after Titmuss had
argued publicly that university professors did not need a salary
increase, another professor declared that Titmuss would not
be content until every spastic was riding around in a Rolls
Royce. I don't think many people found more critical things
than that to say of him.

The other large department, Sociology, is more difficult to
stereotype, partly because it was, and remains, an obstinately
heterogeneous department, and partly because it was the
department in which I was a student and thus more able to
perceive its characteristics in detail. Time has not made it
any easier to acquire a more distant perspective. I have been a
member of that department for the past few years and am
unable now to separate student memories of it from current
reality.

A more powerful source of the ambiguously conservative
atmosphere at LSE resulted from causes only directly political.
The School occupied and still occupies a curiously marginal
position in British public life, despite the involvement of many
of its senior staff with Whitehall, industry and the mass media.
In this country the rank of an institution of higher education
is still measured in relation to Oxford and Cambridge. It is
notable that for a long time LSE has been in the curious position
of being rated more highly internationally than within Britain.
This was revealed strikingly when the LSE, not untypically,
secured the distinguished German, Professor Ralf Dahrendorf,

himself a former student, as its current director. Ironically, the response of many people in this country was, 'What does someone like him want to go to a place like that for?'

An institution can respond to marginality in two ways. It can revel in the role of provocative outsider—and there has always been a minority at LSE which has enjoyed playing this part. Alternatively it can pursue respectability by the extremity of its good behaviour. In a crisis it has been in the latter direction that the weight of opinion in the LSE has leaned. It is an understandable course of action—pursuit of acceptance and stability—but one towards which there are particular pressures in the School. As I have already mentioned, a significant number of the School's leading figures have been central European refugees from Nazism, Fascism, Communism and other sources of intolerance. For them the pursuit of security somewhere in the world has been a particularly high priority. Of course, a place like LSE is bound constantly to disappoint such hopes. No one can expect to bring 3,000 young people together from all over the world, put them in the middle of one of the world's most important cities, set them to work studying the foundations of human society, government, knowledge, economy, and not find them critical, rebellious, questioning, unwilling to be ordered about. To study the social sciences is to demystify the world, to pull away the veneer that conceals the stuff of which authority and social order are really made. And that will usually make for a radicalism of one kind or another.

I do not think it is nostalgia that makes me claim LSE life was a hothouse of political discussion. Events in the outside world could always find a rapid and deeply felt response among us. There was always someone around whose special topic of study covered the event concerned; no place was so remote that there was not someone at LSE whose country it was and for whom things happening there were of major consequence. In particular I remember the way in which we all reacted to the Six-Day War in 1967. Many different groups held agitated and vehement meetings, and while the large numbers of Jewish and Arab students lent the matter urgency, the excitement and serious interest seemed to encompass everybody.

To say that the social sciences necessarily breed Left-wing politics is naive and clearly inaccurate; they are, however, hostile to unquestioning orthodoxy. And thus the two aspects of LSE's personality continue: the search for respectability and the radicalism that comes from scrutiny. These generate the intensive climate of argument over substantial matters which characterizes the School at its best, and occasionally (as in the late 1960s) causes active conflict.

So if the School's political complexities puzzled me when I arrived there as an undergraduate in 1965, I was not disappointed in my expectations of intellectual and political excitement. It was a period when one could be particularly excused for thinking the pursuit of knowledge to be associated with radicalism. Those were the days when 13 years of Conservative rule were being criticized for neglecting the development of science and technology and for the sheer lack of manpower trained in the social sciences within the machinery of government: the days of Sir Alec Douglas-Home's matchsticks and Harold Wilson's slide-rule.

My own motivations in going to the School had been straightforward. I had left school at 17 with no clear aims; I had enjoyed study up to Advanced level GCE (in English, German and Russian) but had no particular interest in pursuing these subjects further. Although a small group of pupils at my school had studied economics and British Constitution, I had no real conception that such a thing as the social sciences existed, though in retrospect I now realize topics in that area in fact interested me. After I had worked for a few years as a journalist writing about industrial safety and, later, local government, I realized it was possible to study academically the things that interested me in society. I was also becoming increasingly aware that I had not educated myself to the extent of my potentialities and was likely to become bored in any job available to me in the foreseeable future. At the age of 21 I began to formulate concrete ambitions for the first time. I decided I wanted to become a Labour Member of Parliament and judged that a knowledge of the social sciences would be a useful asset. In the meantime I was interested in a career in town planning and, believing sociology to be a badly neglected field of knowledge among planners, I thought I would try to enter that profession after acquiring a sociology degree.

For the latter ambition I was too early; for the former too late. I should have had the tenacity to work at the relevance of sociology for planning, because shortly after I turned away from that scheme there was a great flowering of relevant work. But it was not to be found in the literature I encountered in my studies, and my attention was soon distracted by other themes.

On the day after the 1966 General Election I decided it was too late to continue my ambition of becoming an MP. The influence of my friends on the extreme left at LSE was beginning to work on me. What really was the role of parliamentary representatives in social change? What did agencies like Parliament really represent? What was the Labour Party about? I didn't accept the particular answers which my friends offered to these questions, but the questions themselves were enough to disturb the simple certainties which were necessary to maintain me in the confident path I had worked out for myself.

I mention this to illustrate again the way in which, for those of us deeply involved in the politics of LSE, national and international events, local events at the school, our studies and our personal philosophies all intermingled and fused in the same set of issues and questions. The collapse of the Labour Government's economic policy in July 1966 raised the question:

how on earth do the forces of the left mobilize any power at all?
And we tried to give a local answer when we called a sit-in to
resist a decision of the School authorities which we disliked.
What can we *do* about Rhodesia? we asked when we tired of
the fatuity of passing resolutions and marching on Rhodesia
House after the unilateral declaration of independence in
November 1965. The only answer to hand was to resist the
appointment of someone from that country, however remote
from its régime, as Director of the LSE. The nature of authority;
what one was to do about it; the mechanisms of participation
that might be installed in place of the puny and co-opted
systems of representation that the world offered to us as
democracy; these were the concerns that motivated that
initial revolt.

Beyond national concerns the central external issue on which
the rage of most radicals against established powers focused
was Vietnam. Here the large number of American students at
LSE was particularly important. There was also the more
general revulsion against what then seemed to be an industrial
society pursuing the technical rationality of a narrowly-
conceived economic growth at the expense of all other human
values. This fuelled resistance and revolt among students at
most significant universities throughout and beyond the western
world. It also generated the counter-culture, the use of
hallucinogenic drugs and the challenge to technical rationality
in ways that went far beyond the political.

Those who would account for the troubles of the late 1960s
as something local to LSE, to be explained in terms of such factors
as the ugliness of the buildings, the crowded conditions in the
library or the difficulties commonly experienced in trying to
find the lavatories, neglect the universal context. It is true that
in general the student movement eventually became wrapped
in its own causes, borne along by reactions against the authorities'
last reactions to the students' last reactions, but in its central
motivation it was the response of a generation to the political
and economic conditions of its time. And while its impact on

politics has been negligible, its influence on the culture, values and attitudes of that generation has been profound. To the extent that today personal relations are less formal than those of 15 years ago, authority deferred to less automatically and made to justify its actions, the logic of government and industry more often challenged, the forces at work in the student revolts of the late 1960s have been among the causes of the change. And within this country many of the initial stirrings, barely perceived and understood at the time, were to be felt in the growing tensions among the students of the LSE.

I remember the early discussions in which some of us formulated the demand for student participation which was an important early rallying cry, and in particular some meetings at the end of 1966 with a group of senior members of the School who were trying to find out what was developing among us. One of our spokesmen, a graduate student called Ben Brewster, formulated what has since become a familiar slogan, but which was fresh and new at the time: 'People must take part in all decisions which affect their lives'. I remember watching the then Director, Sir Sydney Caine, responding to this. It was a principle which he simply could not begin to concede; it had no place in the free-market liberal democracy to which he held, and there was no way in which he could even discuss the idea.

Then, when the sit-ins and protests came, there were the difficult decisions that a confrontation with authority brings. It was not easy for us young people, for whom arrival at LSE constituted some kind of achievement on the basis of which we might gain others, to defy the symbols and tones of authority to which we normally gave more or less unthinking obedience. And in view of the massive and hostile publicity our actions received, it also meant flying in the face of expressed opinion all around us. Yet large numbers of students joined the protests. In the process we created our defence mechanisms: the closely-knit group bound together in its conspiracy, the elaboration of criteria of judgement which rendered those of the outside world redundant. It led in the end to an extreme and hopeless rigidity; but it also fostered values of scepticism towards authority and suspicion of its motives, an awareness of the operation of power and its cynicism, and a willingness to risk defiance when more or less on our own. These are particular qualities which I have come to identify as the LSE character. It survives youth in the form of a certain kind of toughness, a robust and rather healthy, if slightly paranoid, scepticism, a refusal to submit to hierarchies. I can see it as a product of those years, but I have also seen it in LSE graduates of earlier decades, and it stems ultimately from that laying bare of the foundations of social order which an education in the social sciences necessarily involves. As I have mentioned, our academic studies and our protests fed on each other. These qualities of the 'LSE character' are unfashionable now, in a world where exceptional stress must apparently be placed on the obedient performance of functions within an industrial hierarchy. But they remain the values in which human freedom and dignity are rooted in a hostile world, and I am glad I had them imparted to me.

My personal experience of the 'troubles' gave me, however, something more complex and ambiguous than an induction into rebelliousness. While I was the first person to present (unsuccessfully) a motion to the Students' Union calling on it to boycott lectures and classes shortly before our first protests in Michaelmas Term 1966, I was trying by 1968 (also unsuccessfully) to lead student opposition to the continuing unrest. The constant factor was my ongoing involvement in 'student politics'. This resulted partly from a personal tendency to become involved in the politics and controversies of whatever institutions I become associated with, and partly the result of personal friendships. The president of the Students' Union when I started at the School was Alan Evans (now an officer of the National Union of Teachers). I had met Alan by chance at a Young Fabian weekend school in the year when I was trying to make decisions about going to university. He had encouraged me to apply to the School and had later invited me to look over the place. It was very largely Alan's enthusiasm that led me to LSE, so it was natural to join his circle of friends when I got there. Most of them were involved in Union affairs, and as times changed and people moved on, there remained a little knot of students of my own year and students following us who shared similar though changing views. We remained a close group throughout our undergraduate careers, though only patches of the network now survive. Among them were Jimmie Beck, Chris Brown, Steve Goban, Pippa Jones, Francis Keohane, Pete Lane, Peter Watherston and Joan Freedman (now my wife). In adult life we have become, variously, academics, a civil servant, an industrial manager, a local government officer, a minister of religion (via a merchant bank), a police officer, and a university administrator.

Together we shared in the protests of 1966 and 1967, and together most of us later came to feel that the movement was going too far, was no longer pursuing a reasonable aim of increased student participation, and was in danger of wrecking an institution to which we were committed. We therefore became the nucleus of what were known, though we never chose the title, as the 'moderates' during the upheavals of 1968 and 1969. No doubt temperament and judgement pushed us along that path, but a number of us were in fact impelled some way along it by an event which happened early on when we were still very active in support of the protests. This was on January 31, 1967 when a porter of the School, Mr Ted Poole, collapsed and died a few feet from me in the midst of a ferocious demonstration. Although there was no question of his having been struck by anyone, the scene gave me a glimpse of the potential terror of large numbers of people stirred up by anger and emotion. We were to see a lot more behaviour of that kind and I began to doubt whether the issues at stake really were worth it.

In 1967 my friend Peter Watherston stood successfully for the Presidency of the Union and there were some months of quiet as he tried to negotiate measures for student participation. This activity diverted the attention of the more extreme radicals, even though their objective was really to raise demands which they knew could never be conceded, in order to radicalize the student body further. All the old debates about reform versus revolution became live immediate issues.

It had seemed to me throughout that a natural corollary of being so active in the Union was to try to become President myself, and now there was the added reason that I wanted to try to mobilize students who, while still raising demands for participation, would oppose the extremists. Peter, a Left-wing Tory, had managed a skilful balancing act, staying on good terms with the radicals while conceding them very little. By the time my turn came it was clear that I was more of an intellectual than a politician: I wanted to win the argument rather than the political victories. Instinctively (it is only now that I can see what I was actually doing) I waged the whole thing as an ideological struggle—no quarter given or asked. The election campaign was carried on successfully that way, and shortly afterwards I contributed two articles on student radicalism to *The Guardian*. On the personal level it was all immensely enjoyable: lots of activity, a feeling that I was engaged in something with real meaning and an absence of any real personal bitterness despite the controversy. Virtually no day was purely routine: there were always excuses for long hours of plotting and conspiring in pubs and coffee houses.

I believe I held the support of something more substantial than a notional 'silent majority' throughout the period, but my term of office had one major failing. Although I continued, and with some success, to negotiate student participation with the School, I had really lost interest in acting as the political representative of those to whom I was responsible. As tensions mounted over various issues I was too engrossed in defending the university as an institution against the attacks from the Left to voice student concerns. There was a further problem; given the usual tendency for extremists to attend Union meetings in disproportionate numbers it was becoming impossible to get my policies adopted by the Union.

Resignation became an attractive course of action. Partly it marked a preference for falling rather than being pushed (an increasingly likely alternative); partly it provided an opportunity to regain the initiative in the argument within the student body at large, which seemed more important than staying in office and achieving nothing; finally it forced the extremists to test their strength in an election and not just at Union meetings—something which in the past they had always refused to do. I therefore resigned, along with all those members of the Union Council who supported my position, and in the subsequent election my friend Francis Keohane beat the extremists' candidate to win a few brief weeks' respite for moderation.

That, briefly, was the politics of my experience. Equally important in my memory stand the actions of many involved outside a political context. There were few at LSE happy with the fierce oppositions developing; after all it was a quarrel between teachers and students at a highly selective and élite institution. The instincts of most were for agreement, rapprochement. And many people devoted themselves desperately to that task, sacrificing their equanimity, dignity and emotional resources in the process. It was both touching and disturbing to see so many people losing the poise that normally disguised their more inward feelings and responses. Some, among them men of major intellectual stature, became so enraged at the protests that they virtually lost control of their judgement and were unable to wield the power that they believed should be used.

Certain barriers between teachers and students were broken down in the process, and I remember thinking at the time that from then on relations between these two groups would henceforth be more open and, curiously, friendly. At the level of personal contacts I think I was right, but there was something else I did not anticipate and have only noticed more recently as a teacher observing my colleagues. While the attitude of academics towards students whom they know is almost without exception generous, kindly and responsible, many of them have developed a hostility, a curious mixture of lese-majesty and churlishness, in their response to the demands of students in the mass—or sometimes to the mere idea of students in the mass. It is one of the continuing unfortunate legacies of the troubles of the late 1960s.

But behind all the displays of emotion during our troubles stood men and women who understood the operation of power and waited coolly for the right moment to wield it. On the student side these were nearly always US or South African students who were really fighting the more extreme and bitter conflicts of their own countries in the confines of what was still in many ways a restrained English affair. (I recall, during the fearsome national Vietnam demonstration in Trafalgar Square, October 1968, Jim Callaghan, the Home Secretary, and his junior minister Shirley Williams, chatting to groups of the demonstrators.)

On the School side a small baronial group of senior academic staff similarly guided events. In fact, the authorities' handling of the troubles matured as time passed. In 1966 and 1967 they saw the whole thing as outrageous disobedience which should be checked by firm discipline. That phase was symbolized in the very human figure of the then School Secretary, Mr Harry Kidd, displaying a down-to-earth anger and muttering about the lessons of Munich and Appeasement. By 1969 the situation had been fully recognized as a straight conflict between two sides, and there was no more talk of discipline. The game was politics. The Director, the late Sir Walter Adams, did not relish this kind of situation. His conception of liberalism—embodied in his work for academic Jewish refugees during the last war and in his attempt to run a multi-racial college in Rhodesia—had been rejected by the radical students

—and now his gentlemanly model of how a university authority should behave was being rendered useless by the urgencies of the hour. I remember seeing him once when a possibly dangerous sit-in was imminent. He wanted to anticipate it by closing the School in advance; but an announcement of the closure would itself precipitate the sit-in. The idea of closing the School without prior warning was in his view out of the question.

One of the key figures in the School's decisions at this time was in fact a relatively junior member of staff, Dr Bernard Donoughue, who happened to be one of the academics serving a period on the Court of Governors. He was among the few people who, while actively engaged in events, remained on good personal terms with virtually every faction, at the same time maintaining a clear sense of the circumstances under which the School authorities should shift from compromise and accommodation to strong action and discipline. He has recently left the School to serve as senior policy adviser to both Sir Harold Wilson and Mr Callaghan. Recalling his skills during the LSE affair, I often feel that the short-term future of the Labour Government must be more securely based than it seems.

With all that politics, did any work ever get done? is a question I was often asked by outsiders. As I have already said, in many ways the concerns of the protests mingled fruitfully with those of our studies. (I remember one of the leading radicals, David Adelstein, infuriating academics by telling them that the protests provided a kind of experimental laboratory for students of the social sciences.) Eventually, especially in 1969 when the School buildings were closed for several weeks during the Lent term, the negative effect of it all could be seen in examination results and similar indicators. However, it is also true that the troubles spared our generation from some traditional LSE student complaints. In my first year—before the troubles and hence more typical of normal LSE—we complained of the unfriendliness of the place, of feelings of isolation, the difficulty of joining existing student activities (most of which were firmly in the control of cliques), the tendency for the place to be empty in the evenings. The troubles temporarily changed all that. An intensive activity, a set of urgent, shared concerns, created a strong sense of community. Cliques became irrelevant as a completely new pattern of activities developed. Various parts of the buildings themselves, usually so bland and institutional, acquired a significance beyond themselves: the Old Theatre where most of urgent Students' Union debates took place; Florrie's coffee bar, the George IV and the White Horse where conspiratorial, or anxious, or simply gossipy groups gathered; the Students' Union offices where the duplicating machines daily churned out manifestos and ephemera, proving there, as elsewhere, as crucial to the student revolt as the printing press was to the Reformation.

In more normal times complaints about the social life of the School return. Closely related to the charges of unfriendliness are those concerning LSE's philistinism which probably results from the absence of literature and arts students within such a specialized institution. In the 1960s a Drama Society did in fact still flourish but it has since passed away, a victim of the crisis in Students' Union finance, its own particular quarrels and the larger ones of the troubles themselves.

There is, in fact, as one would expect from a place housing many people of mathematical ability, a fair amount of music at the School. Yet it also appears a submerged activity. Music and the arts in general seem unable to advance beyond the margins of LSE communal life, despite the efforts throughout its history of Mrs Bernard Shaw, Lady Beveridge and countless staff and students. The Shaw Library remains a delightful oasis but a very contained one. And despite my own deep attachments to the School, whenever in the choir and orchestra we send the strains of, say, the Mozart Requiem down through those endless gaunt corridors and staircases, I feel part of a group of trespassers temporarily taking possession of and gentling that urgent and intense institution with a part of human existence which its own priorities and values, vital and relevant though they are, cannot encompass.

Frederic C. Weiss

Frederic C. Weiss was born in 1953 in New York City. Having attended Rutgers College for two years, he graduated from the University of Massachusetts in 1975, summa cum laude. *He spent the 1976–77 academic year working towards his M.Sc. in Social Administration at the London School of Economics.*

olitics and writing have, for some years, been two of my greatest, though not exclusive, passions. During our twenties we are supposed to decide what we want to do with our lives, as if by deciding we can make it happen. In the summer of 1976 I had to make a decision. Having applied for and been awarded a Rotary Foundation Graduate Fellowship to the London School of Economics I had the chance to study in Europe for a year. As I had already passed up a seat in law school the previous year there was considerable pressure by my family to give up my Fellowship and start law school. 'Life goes by very quickly and you should get on with it,' my father said.

Yet I decided to go to the LSE. I don't think I left the USA to come over to Europe as an all-expenses-paid escape, but rather as an adventure. I came with a sense of hope, a curiosity about the intricacy and the philosophy of the Welfare State. I was vaguely aware of the reputation of the Webbs, Laski and Beveridge, and thought the LSE would be a good school and London a unique city. Although there were moments during the summer of 1976 when I felt I was being ripped apart by my own diverse aspirations, the decision to come to the LSE was never meant to be a substitute for writing; rather an intellectual supplement and a personal odyssey.

My first day at the School, still suffering from jet-lag, I

settled down for an afternoon tea, and perused *The Times*
looking for the score of the New York Yankees baseball play-
off games. When I couldn't find the score in the newspaper, it
finally sank into my brain just how far I really was from home.
Putting down my newspaper, I looked up and first noticed the
posters. They told me to get my money out of South Africa;
to get out of Northern Ireland; to join the victory of the
workers in China; not to wear Chilean shoes; not to bank at
Barclay's; and much more.

A school can be characterized by its most vital activity:
LSE by the energy of political passion represented by such
posters. The rhetoric of 'relative deprivation', or 'Marxian
economics' is used at all levels from class lectures to small talk
at the pub. Some friends were only *half* joking when they
walked up to attractive women at the *Beaver's Retreat* and asked
if they had 'read any good books about Strategic Arms Limitations lately?' Or, as one of my friends, West Coughlin once
said, 'Back in the States, when guys got together over a beer,
they'd talk about cars and girls, here they talk about macro-
economic theory, or international communism.'

While sexual encounters at the LSE are minimal, intellectual
and geographical encounters are easy to find. There are students
from almost every country in the world and this can be
fascinating. For instance, there are the Chinese students who
are for the most part hard-working, interesting, and most
personable. Their sartorial trimmings are the standard Maoist
suit that won't change much through the years as they go to
work for the Government, and in some cases rise to the top
of the Government. Yet, sometimes watching some of my
fellow students from the USA, still dressed quite leisurely in
well-worn jeans and comfortable sweaters, approach the
Chinese students in conversation, it has struck me how this
was becoming the very 'in' thing to do. It is, in many ways,
very 'UN', to know one of the Chinese students by his or her
first name, and no doubt it confirms many students' own,
long-term career goals (dreams) of meeting these same Chinese

students many years from now across a conference table, solving the problems of the world.

Less than a hundred years old, the LSE's reputation, while quite respectable around the world, is still in its primary stages compared with Oxford and Cambridge. The LSE has a 'guerrilla' campus; its students and faculty come together from all over the city during the day, before dispersing into the camouflage of greater London. There is no easily defined 'academic community' at the LSE. You'll find very few students walking around with their LSE scarves wrapped comfortably around their necks (although they do exist), and if you walk away from the inconspicuous passage way on Houghton Street that leads to the group of LSE buildings (connected by umbilical cord passageways in the air), you can meet dozens of people from all walks of life who have no idea that the LSE is even there at all.

At times I think I would have preferred the security and close camaraderie of Oxford or Cambridge. Some evenings I have walked out of the library exhausted and lonely, and been depressed by the empty streets. Where did all the people go? Where did they run to? The porters still remained to add a sense of order and stability, but they looked tired and bored. In some ways, I'll remember LSE for the faces of people who pass by, but whose names I do not know; people whom I've talked to once over coffee and hoped to meet again but who have vanished for weeks at a time. None of us slows down long enough to get to know more than a dozen or so people well enough to call friends.

Still, it is exciting to know that there are so many people around; and that at any given minute during the day there are at least two classes going on that I would like to sit in on. This aggravates my tutor, Mike Reddin, a brilliant and sympathetic fellow, no end. He is an enthusiastic lecturer in Social Administration and tolerates all my moods of academic wandering and occasional fits of intellectual paralysis. He just keeps pushing books about the British Welfare State my way, and saying, 'Don't believe all the myths about the Welfare State that you read in the daily papers; keep reading and questioning things, and get behind the myths.' Reddin, who served as the late Richard Titmuss's research assistant when Titmuss was a mainstay of the Social Administration Department, is always willing to sit down over a beer and debate the concepts of 'Universal' versus 'Selective' benefits, or just go over still another revision in my thesis topic. At a school that is often intimidating and sometimes impersonal, Reddin adds a touch of the human element.

During this year at LSE I've gone through my share of low moments, wondering if I'm learning enough and what it is all going to lead to in the end, and asking myself what do I want to do with my life anyway? One evening, walking home after a particularly discouraging night in the library, I stopped outside the Aldwych Theatre, attracted by the gaiety of the people strolling outside for a breath of air during the inter-mission. Towering above the crowd was John Kenneth Galbraith. I approached him, introduced myself and explained that I had done an extensive research project on his work during my senior year at college. When he asked me what I was doing, I explained that I was studying at the LSE for a year. He was restrained but polite and said that he had spent some time at the LSE many years ago. He named a few professors who used to teach at the School when he was there, and asked if I knew them. Not having heard of any of them I noted that 'they're probably dead by now.' Professor Galbraith nodded and then he said, 'Yes, they probably are.' As excited as I was to be talking to him, the sadness of the moment did not escape me. To be reminded of mortality must make even the famous feel vulnerable and pensive. We exchanged small talk for a few minutes, but clearly there was little else to say. When the flashing light signalled that the second act was about to commence, Galbraith excused himself and went back to his seat.

Politics at the LSE are too simplistic and a bit too ideological and dogmatic for my tastes. Important student policy is determined at sparsely-attended Union meetings, democratic in principle, but in reality most unrepresentative. Small but well disciplined groups have an influence far beyond their actual support on the campus. The simplicity of the Left disturbed me from the start of the term. Often certain Leftist groups are so committed to ideological dogma that they lose all credibility. If you listened to them all year, you could be convinced that the CIA is behind every crisis in the world including the strike at Leyland, but that the KGB is a radio station in Birmingham. After a few months I decided not to get upset about the ideological acrobatics going on at the LSE. I went about building up my own defence, a 'bourgeois' cynical sense of humour.

When the French released Abu-Daoud, the alleged organizer of the massacre of Israeli athletes in Munich, the whole world was buzzing. But in the halls of the LSE, there was not a sign of outrage. The posters condemning injustice in outer Mongolia, or calling for the liberation of the North Pole were still on the walls. But the political movements didn't feel at all moved by the release of Abu-Daoud. When I ran into some friends outside St Clement's building, we wondered what would happen if we put up posters protesting the release of Abu-Daoud, and announcing a silent protest in the courtyard. The purpose would not be to see how many people showed up, but rather how many posters would still be on the walls by the end of the day. We never went through with the plan but looking back at it, perhaps we should have.

What makes me so cynical about politics at the LSE goes beyond ideological disagreements. The origin of my cynicism is that so much of the radical political consciousness is simple play acting: building up an enemy where no enemy exists, so that you can organize a united front to oppose 'it'; trying to keep the press out of the Union meetings during an occupation of the administrative building, unless they are certified as 'sympathetic' to the students; maintaining the occupation

after being served with a court order to vacate; agreeing not to
resist police action to remove them from the building, but
refusing to open the door.

The result of this great moment of political strategy was
that last February several hundred extra police had to come to
the LSE and hack the doors down in Connaught House, only to
find friendly students ready to vacate without force or non-
violent resistance (like sitting on the floor and making all the
over-time police earn their money by carrying them out). It
was neither a peaceful surrender, nor a dedicated and last
ditch resistance. It was, for lack of a better word, play acting.
Some of my friends who had seen the most vigorous anti-war
demonstrations back in the United States chuckled at this
occupation at the 'radical hotbed' LSE.

But a cynical sense of humour is only one of the many
things that the LSE has helped me develop. Between Michael
Reddin and Brian Abel-Smith I have been given a much wider
view of the issues surrounding the formation of social policy
in the modern technocracy. Brian Abel-Smith rushes from class
to Whitehall, teaching his humble pupils both at the LSE and
in the Labour Government how the Welfare State *should* be
run. Sometimes he seems distracted, other times a bit bored,
and now and then exhausted, but he is always knowledgeable
and fascinating to listen to.

Not all of my courses are as satisfying, but over all, being at
the London School of Economics has helped me understand
the functions, the needs and the aims of the Welfare State.
More than ever I realize how complicated some of the problems
facing modern society are, and some of the steps that must be
taken in the years ahead.

But even if I learned nothing in my courses, the year at the
LSE would still be a valuable experience in a personal sense.
There are things that I have gained that have nothing to do
with exams or essays. They aren't things that can be graded,
perhaps even fully expressed. They are things that you take

with you, long after you are not one of the familiar faces around the hall way.

In January 1977, when the IRA declared 'war on London' and bombed several stores on Oxford Street to prove it, I ran into Mark Stewart, another student from the United States. Mark brought up the topic of the IRA bombings, and said that he wasn't very scared at the LSE because he figured that the IRA would know that 'we're not the enemy'. Mark was joking, and it was funny at the time. But he was also close to the truth. The LSE is like an independent nation, with its own diplomatic relations and foreign policy. Perhaps it could have joined the United Nations, if it didn't have a population that went home to the city of London every night.

Krishendath Maharaj

Krishendath Maharaj was born in Rio Claro, Trinidad, on 15 June, 1957. He was educated there and at Presentation College, San Fernando. He spent a year at the University of the West Indies before coming to LSE in 1976.

My parents were first generation Indian immigrants to Trinidad. Born in 1957, the fifth of seven children, I was moulded by the unreal world of the Trinidadian Hindu—a world that blindly clings to taboos and rituals as expressions of identity in a tense, diverse society. At the very outset my education was viewed as an escape route—a means to economic and social improvement. The stark poverty of my surroundings provided a spur to achievement and a constant reminder of the consequences of failure.

My father was a labourer—repairing pot-holes in the road; my mother was a sempstress. It may seem extraordinary that in addition to the economic burden of feeding seven mouths they should undertake the daunting cost of educating their children. But they were brave, and perhaps foolish, so that when my eldest brother, after six years at primary school, obtained a limited scholarship to secondary school, very little deliberation on principle was necessary.

He went off to school, and a precedent had been set; in turn my brothers and my sister followed him. By the time I was ready to go, the financial difficulties had been slightly eased by the employment of my two eldest brothers. The very fact that so much sacrifice was necessary to educate us inculcated a deep sense of obligation and responsibility, and moreover added to the pressure to do well. But I always hated school. I was frustrated, sometimes to the point of desperation by the tedious hours, the grim, joyless teachers, the fruitless regurgitation of force-fed facts, yet I was determined to survive and fulfil my teachers' expectations.

The passing of 'O' levels created no feeling of achievement for there was never any possibility of opting out at any stage. It was merely a continuation of mechanically attempting to satisfy the hopes and aspirations of others. My performance at 'O' levels, however, indicated that I stood the chance of gaining one of the very few national awards given at 'A' levels. These national awards enable the holder to study at any university in the world, with all fees paid. Now, while my teachers, hopeful for the prestige which my success would bring to the school, impressed on me the need to study hard, for the first time I consciously strove to excel on my own behalf. An award would mean freedom, the ability to choose; an entirely new life would be open to me.

So I did well. And I won an award. And I came to LSE.

My choice of LSE from the wide range of alternatives was intimately bound up with the constraints of my Trinidadian education. I expected LSE to supply all that my previous educational experience had lacked. My study of Economics at 'A' level had already constituted a minor revolt against the usual streaming of the more successful into study of the sciences. LSE's reputation, academically, suggested a continuation of study in a field which absorbed me increasingly—and besides, it was a British university and therefore 'good'. The possibility of travel, of leaving Trinidad for a foreign country, in itself was exciting, but most enticing of all was LSE's political reputation. A friend who had been attending LSE informed me conspiratorially that LSE was 'Marxist', and my Spanish teacher said, 'LSE? Ah yes, Laski and the communists, eh?' The chance of being at the centre of intellectual and social revolt, where I would see real, live communists, was too good to miss!

During the year after 'A' levels, I attended lectures at the University of the West Indies, and the appalling similarity of student life there to secondary school left me with a thankful sense that LSE was going to be different. There I would find none of the limitations and absurd competitiveness I had so far experienced. LSE, I was confident, would be a place of advanced learning, discussion and dissent. The students would all be aware and active, participating together with their lecturers in the life of the community. How far this was from the truth I discovered only upon arrival.

My first contact with a sample of the student body was at the Freshers' Conference. Everyone had a little button with his name on it, but I arrived late, didn't get the button, and felt lost and lonely without it. I couldn't find my host so I retreated into a corner and looked around at the lively crowd. No one else seemed to be lonely, so I eased myself into a little group and was immediately astonished at the range of nationalities and accents. Everyone appeared very bright and intent on impressing each other with their knowledge of art, literature and music. My opinion of myself plunged considerably. A tiny Kuwaiti girl, dressed in black, with a chain of prayer beads, fascinated me, so I struck up a conversation. Gradually I relaxed, and soon entered into a heated argument with a Mauritian (later to be my next-door neighbour and close friend) about the concept of violence being inherent in the state. I had become one of them.

The next day we all went to LSE where we were duly impressed with our good fortune at being there. The first thing that struck me was the smallness and the age of the LSE building in which, however, I managed to lose myself with remarkable ease. To my surprise the students seemed to be quite preoccupied with getting booklists, etc., but I thought this must be a condition peculiar to freshers; the real excitement would come when I met the experienced students, those veterans of political strife who had rejected the arbitrary confines of books and would lead the way to intellectual nirvana. I wandered around joining societies and saying 'Hi!' to all and sundry. Suddenly I saw a stall for the International Marxist Group.

There at last! A real live communist! Unfortunately she was just a vaguely pretty girl, quite unlike my expectation of a dishevelled, barefoot, bra-less, drop-out revolutionary. Instead of urging me to support the struggle of the proletariat, she just smiled and asked if I was a fresher. I began having twinges of doubt.

In spite of exhortations by the School to mix freely among all students, I found it far easier to relax in non-white company—it simply required too much effort to attune myself to the wavelength of the typical British student. Besides, my neighbours in the hall of residence were foreigners who happened to be doing the same courses so few further contacts were made through my studies. As I tried to expand my life, I came into contact with friends whose backgrounds intrigued me—so much of our experience was different, yet so much was the same. At the very beginning of term, I was befriended, separately, by a small, dark, totally independent Mauritian girl, and a mysterious, distant Kenyan undergraduette. They turned out to be the closest of friends and together shaped much of my subsequent life at LSE through fascinating discussions over endless cups of tea and coffee in the crowded, noisy refectory—the only place where people can meet in LSE.

Initially, I attended all my lectures and classes and did the recommended reading and exercises. It dawned on me that I was behaving like a typical 'A' level swotter—life at LSE was supposed to be different! I saw lecturers only at lectures where they dispensed notes and proceeded to read through them over an hour-long period. I fell asleep with alarming alacrity. My puzzlement and disillusionment grew. Where, I asked myself, was the lively, interrelated community of lecturers and students? My personal tutor I saw for five minutes—the benefits of such a system still escape me. The academics existed in a separate world and seemed completely divorced from me and everyone else. The only human character was my Maths tutor, a lanky, sandy-haired American, forever puffing at an unlit pipe. He was the epitome of the crazy mathematician going into ecstasies over infinity, but genuinely bewildered at our inability to solve his problems which he later confessed were beyond him as well.

As for the LSE student body it seemed to consist of a surprisingly apolitical, apathetic mass. The main—if not only—aim seemed to be the attainment of a degree, to the exclusion of any extracurricular activity. The first indication I had that students did other things besides study came at the first Students' Union meeting of term. The question of rising and discriminatory fees for overseas students was raised by a Sikh in a red turban. When he mentioned racism a highly-charged discussion ensued which at last gave me an experience to recall and relish, and was in effect the impetus for involvement in the fee campaign. When, one day, a lanky Pakistani handed me a leaflet bearing the magic word 'discrimination' I was hooked instantly and discovered that the Overseas Students Action Committee could provide a welcome forum for my frustrated political activities.

Quickly absorbing the necessary skills of drafting inflammatory leaflets, operating the leaflet duplicator, designing and putting up posters, I became a fully-fledged activist whose task was to bring enlightenment to the masses about the threat to a major part of the student body caused by rising fees. The process of education consisted of slipping news-sheets under doors, talking to people, getting petitions signed and in general forcing the students to consider the issues. Interestingly enough, the weekly Students' Union meeting hardly ever provided a platform for us as it was dominated by a relatively small number of students devoted to irrelevant and inbred politics. But my involvement in the Overseas Students' Action Committee brought me face to face with the Director of the School, Ralf Dahrendorf. Instead of a bristly, tough, barely-reformed Nazi-type oppressor, he appeared to be a slight, wispy character, though he was perhaps more wily than I suspected.

The first stirrings of militant activity occurred in November

1976 when some top officials of the oppressive Indonesian regime were invited to a seminar by Michael Leiger of the International Relations Department. A hundred or so students rushed upstairs and blockaded the seminar room and after an hour-long vigil punctuated by hammering on the door and cries of 'Murderers Out!' the Indonesians finally left. At last my faith in the character of LSE students was partially restored.

The big issue, however, remained the fee campaign. In the second term the Administration prepared to ratify increases at an Academic Board meeting in early February. We decided to organize a mass meeting of students at the same time and I was amazed at the turn-out—a large gathering of about 800 students. Such was the tension and excitement we all realized an occupation was inevitable. For two hours we listened to speakers and watched a film—*Salt of the Earth*—while we nervously and impatiently awaited the return of a student delegation which had been admitted to the Board meeting. The lights went up; the film died in mid frame; the delegation had returned. After the inevitable speeches we flocked out in a massive stream to Connaught House. I was caught up in the throng, and my initial slight misgivings were lost in the contagious enthusiasm of the crowd. The occupation began.

The interplay of forces during the occupation was a fascinating spectacle for me. I helped coordinate a massive publicity campaign: leaflets for and against littered the refectory tables and were shoved upon indifferent students at the main entrances; posters were put up and ripped down; the Director himself printed leaflets and put up posters. An air of routine quickly supervened and listlessness due to lack of sleep and fresh air constantly threatened, though the possibility of police intervention and challenge to student autonomy was a potent stimulus. The political factionalism constantly put the success of the occupation in jeopardy though the daily, massively attended, Students' Union meetings were a witness to confirmed sceptics like me of the level of support in the university. Naturally all this activity involved a considerable sacrifice of attendance at lectures and classes, but I felt that there was no question of priorities; I fully believed that we could achieve success. But after a court injunction was served the occupation lost its original purpose and became a defiance to intimidation more than anything else. This experience and two further minor protests over the fees issue combined to convince me that students, in order to achieve anything in their own sphere, should avoid the factionalisms of the wider political scene and concentrate upon the issues that concern them.

Still, life for me so far at LSE has been a stimulating and vastly educational experience and it is only because I wanted such involvement in student affairs that I can make this claim. It seems to me that there is a deliberate playing down of student activity by the Administration solely in an attempt to reform the image of LSE. To me such a reform would entail a great loss of character and vitality. This is not to say that as an LSE student I felt it incumbent upon me, by reason of tradition, to participate in the life of the School in the manner I did. Rather it is because the yearning for change, for revolt against established values and systems always persists, and finds a freer (better?) expression in a climate which is not actively hostile to it.

At the LSE, the standard isolation of the overseas student is mitigated by the large proportion of foreigners, and it is a credit to the much vaunted 'international flavour' of LSE that I have been so easily able to settle down to a university career which promises to be rich in rewards.